JESUS AND P

JESUS AND PSYCHOLOGY

Edited by
Fraser Watts

DARTON·LONGMAN+TODD

First published in 2007 by
Darton, Longman and Todd Ltd
1 Spencer Court
140-142 Wandsworth High Street
London SW18 4JJ

ISBN-10: 0-232-52709-1
ISBN-13: 978-0-232-52709-4

All biblical references are taken from the New Revised Standard
Version unless otherwise noted

A catalogue record for this book is available from the British Library.

Typeset by YHT Ltd, London
Printed in Great Britain by
The Cromwell Press, Trowbridge, Wiltshire

This book is dedicated to my friends and colleagues at the church of St Edward King and Martyr, Cambridge

Contents

Contributors

Fraser Watts is Director of the Psychology and Religion Research Group at the University of Cambridge, where he is also Reader in Theology and Natural Science. He is a Fellows of Queens' College and Vicar-Chaplain of St Edward's Church in Cambridge. His current research is on development of a cognitive-psychological model of religion, and on the interface of psychology and theology. He is the author of *Science Meets Faith* (1998), *Theology and Psychology* (2002), and co-editor of *Forgiveness in Context* (2004).

Justin J. Meggitt is University Senior Lecturer in the Study of Religion and the Origins of Christianity at the Institute of Continuing Education at Cambridge University and a Fellow of Hughes Hall. His research and teaching focuses mainly on formative Christianity within the context of the early Roman Empire. He is the author of *Paul, Poverty and Survival* (1998).

Liz Gulliford is a research assistant in the Psychology and Religion Research Group. She currently conducts theoretical and empirical research on the psychology and theology of gratitude. She has also published and delivered lectures on the topic of forgiveness, and co-edited *Forgiveness in Context* (2004), with Fraser Watts.

Sara Savage is a Senior Research Associate in the Psychology of Religion Research Group, where she conducts empirical research on religiously motivated violence as well as the interface of psychology and Christian ministry. She is a lecturer in the Cambridge Theological Federation, and her publications include *Psychology for the Christian Ministry* (2001), *Ambiguous Evangelism* (2004), and *Making Sense of Generation Y* (2005).

Beaumont Stevenson is Chaplain of Oxfordshire and Buckinghamshire Mental Healthcare NHS Partnership Trust, an honorary Canon of Christ Church Cathedral, and Advisor on Pastoral Care and Counselling for the Diocese of Oxford. He has taught extensively on the interface between theology and pastoral counselling.

Jesse W. Abell earned his BS in Psychology at Indiana Wesleyan University and read for an MPhil in Psychology and Religion at the University of Cambridge. He subsequently earned his MDiv at the School of the Theology at the University of the South and was ordained to the priesthood in the Episcopal Church (USA). He has presented research at a number of colloquia and research conferences and has published several journal articles. He is a member of the Religious Research Association and the International Association for Cross Cultural Psychology.

James M. Day is Professor in the Faculty of Psychology and Educational Sciences at the Université Catholique de Louvain, Belgium, where he works in the Human Development Laboratory and Psychology of Religion Research Centre; Consulting Psychologist in the Centre de Neuropsychiatrie et de Psychotherapie in Brussels; and Anglican priest serving as Assistant Chaplain at The Pro-Cathedral of The Holy Trinity, Brussels, and the Spiritualité et Vie programme at Louvain. James is co-author and co-editor of *Human Development Across the Lifespan* (2006) (2nd Edition), and his work has appeared in journals including *American Psychologist*, *Human Development*, *Journal of Counseling and Development*, *The Journal of Moral Education*, and the *International Journal for the Psychology of Religion*. He has recently been elected Co-Editor in Chief of the Archiv fur Religionspsychologie, the Journal of the International Association for the Psychology of Religion.

Leslie J. Francis is Director of the Welsh National Centre for Religious Education and Professor of Practical Theology at the University of Wales, Bangor. He received his PhD and ScD from the University of Cambridge, and his DD from the University of Oxford. He is an Anglican priest and Fellow of the British Psychological Society. He is author of *Faith and Psychology* (2005) and is co-author of the *Personality Type and Scripture* series including *Exploring Luke's Gospel* (2000), *Exploring Matthew's Gospel* (2001) and *Exploring Mark's Gospel* (2002).

Everett L. Worthington, Jr., is Professor of Psychology at Virginia Commonwealth University and a licensed clinical psychologist. He conducts empirical research in forgiveness and its application in therapeutic practice, and has directed A Campaign for Forgiveness Research, a non-profit organization that supports and works towards building a field of scientific research in forgiveness studies. His recent publications include *Forgiveness and Reconciliation* (2006), *Handbook of Forgiveness* (2005), *The Power of Forgiveness* (2005), *Hope-focused Marriage* (2005), and *Forgiving and Reconciling* (2003).

Preface

This book shows how psychology can be used in reading and understanding the gospels. It is an important application of psychology both from religious and academic points of view.

For Christians, there is nothing more important than understanding the significance of the life and teaching of Jesus. Psychology can play an important role in that, particularly in grasping the personal significance of Jesus. It is when people gain an insight in to the mind of Jesus, and so understand how his teaching is relevant to them personally, that a life-changing relationship with Jesus develops.

In addition, the academic study of the Bible has benefited enormously in recent years from being pursued in collaboration with other disciplines, including the social sciences and the study of literature. Rather belatedly, psychology is now also making a really significant contribution to the study of the Bible, and this book contributes to that developing project. It looks at the personality of Jesus himself and how it is portrayed, at the psychological significance of his teaching, and at the psychological processes involved in reading the gospels.

I am grateful to the contributors for finding time in busy schedules to contribute chapters to this book. We have worked collaboratively as far as possible, and the majority of the chapters have arisen from work in Cambridge. Three of us (Sara Savage, Liz Gulliford and myself) are based in the Psychology and Religion Research Group in the Faculty of Divinity at the

University of Cambridge. Our chapters arose from talks given at St Edward's Church in Cambridge, where I am Vicar-Chaplain, as did the chapter by Beaumont Stevenson. Another author (Justin Meggitt) is Cambridge-based and has close links with our research group. Three more authors (Everett Worthington, James Day and Jesse Abell) have spent extended periods with us in Cambridge and their chapters arose from those visits.

I am grateful to colleagues in the Psychology and Religion Research Group for help in editing the book, particularly to Bonnie Zahl who has worked carefully through all the chapters in a most conscientious and helpful way, and to Marcus Ramhaw for valuable help at an earlier stage with one particular chapter.

We hope that this book will show how helpful psychology can be in understanding the gospels, and that it will whet people's appetite for more work on the psychological interpretation of the Bible.

Fraser Watts
Queens' College, Cambridge
August 2006

1

Fraser Watts

APPROACHING THE GOSPELS

PSYCHOLOGICALLY

The use of psychology in the interpretation of the Bible has had a chequered history. In nineteenth-century Germany there were a number of prominent attempts to develop a psychological portrait of Jesus. However, it was an enterprise that drew widespread and stringent criticism and it gradually fell into disrepute and was largely abandoned. Several intellectual currents came together to contribute to this abandonment of psychological interpretation of the Bible. It came to be distrusted by scholars concerned with biblical interpretation as going too far beyond the evidence available. Also, in the early part of the twentieth century, psychology itself became narrower and more reductionist, and thus lent itself less readily to being used in biblical interpretation. Thirdly, the psychology of religion, which had been a vigorous field of activity in the early days of modern psychology, experienced a severe decline, and by around 1930 had become a very peripheral part of the discipline.

In recent decades, the situation has changed on all three fronts. Biblical studies have become more interdisciplinary; psychology has become more emancipated; and the psychology of religion has revived. It is worth exploring all three in more detail.

Though the historical and critical study of scriptural texts has remained central to biblical interpretation, it has increasingly been recognised that this does not address all the interesting questions that arise about the Bible, and that there is value in drawing on other disciplines. For example, there has been a good deal of work, from the standpoint of the social sciences, on the culture in which the New Testament was produced. Such work has been widely recognised as enriching our understanding of the New Testament. Also, the Bible has been studied as literature, bringing to bear the resources and methodologies associated with the study of any great work of literature. In the increasingly interdisciplinary climate of biblical studies, there is a recognised place for psychology as well.

Secondly, psychology has become broader. During the middle years of the twentieth century, psychology imposed on itself various restrictions that were assumed to be necessary if it was to have the status of a science. In particular, it was widely assumed that psychology should confine itself to the study of externally observable behaviour, and to proceed by repeatable, experimental observations. However, our understanding of what constitutes a science has broadened, and there has been increasing recognition that not all sciences are the same. Also, psychology has found a way of returning to the study of the mind, with scientific rigour; that has been facilitated by the analogy between the human mind and a computer. The result has been that psychology has become a broader and less rigid discipline than it was a few decades ago.

Thirdly, there has been a revival of the psychology of religion. This has focused less on grand theories of why people are religious, and more on assembling a wealth of fascinating, detailed information about many different facets of religious life. We now know a great deal about topics as varied as mystical experience, conversion, speaking in tongues, how religion develops in children, how religion relates to mental health, amongst others. For the most part, psychology has studied religion from the standpoint of an external observer, but there has also been an increasingly rich interface between psychology and various aspects of theology, including the interpretation of the Bible.

The new climate has led to a striking revival of psychological work on the interpretation of the Bible. It was a reflection of the revival that in 1991 the Society of Biblical Literature established a programme on Psychology and Biblical Studies, and the programme has in turn advanced that revival further. One important product of the programme was a thorough review of psychological work on the Bible so far: *Soul and Psyche: The Bible in psychological perspective* (Rollins, 1999). Five years later this was followed by a four-volume edited work, *Psychology and the Bible* (Ellens and Rollins, 2004) that brings together a total of 62 essays representing the best and most current psychological interpretation of the Scriptures.

Guidelines for Psychological Exegesis

Criticisms made a hundred years ago of psychological interpretation of the Bible often pointed out that psychology was being used in a very amateurish way. The complaint was not so much about the idea of using psychology as an aid to biblical interpretation, but about the methodologies used in practice, which were very unconvincing. As a result of such criticisms, the present climate is more careful, and guidelines have been developed about how psychology can most appropriately be used. Interpreters should be aware of three important guidelines for making psychological interpretations of the Bible.

Firstly, it needs to be recognised that psychology is quite diverse. Indeed, we have a family of different approaches to psychology, rather than a single one. The psychologies of Freud and Jung have probably been used most extensively in biblical interpretation. However, there are many other potentially relevant areas of psychology concerned, for example, with personality, development, cognition and much else. The first volume of *Psychology and the Bible* (Ellens and Rollins, 2004) indicates the range of psychologies that can be used in biblical interpretation.

One key limitation with much psychological interpretation of the Bible is that it has relied completely on one particular approach to psychology, often in an uncritical way.

An awareness of the variety of psychological approaches is helpful in introducing a critical perspective on the use of psychology in reading the Bible. Different approaches have the potential to elucidate different aspects of a particular passage. It is always right to be wary of any claim to have the psychological approach to a particular passage, and more appropriate to see it as one psychological approach among a variety that may be possible. To make this point, some psychological work on the Bible has explicitly used several different psychological approaches in parallel. Most notably, in studying several key passages of St Paul, Gerd Theissen (1987) has made use of behavioural, cognitive and psychodynamic approaches to each passage studied. To illustrate every possible psychological approach to the gospels would take a much longer book than this one, but we have sampled enough areas to at least make the point that there are multiple psychologies that can be brought to bear, not just one.

A second important guideline for the use of psychology in interpreting the Bible is to make good use of what is known in other ways about biblical texts. The ideal is an interdisciplinary enterprise that draws on what is known from more traditional historical-critical approaches to the Bible, but enriches it with a psychological perspective. Such interdisciplinary work is, of course, demanding, and almost anyone approaching it will be better versed either in psychology or biblical criticism. That is just in the nature of any interdisciplinary enterprise such as this, but the inevitable area of weakness of one practitioner will be compensated for by the strengths of someone with a different and complementary background.

Unfortunately, there are some rather glaring examples in the literature of people whose expertise has been in psychology, and who have been clearly been ignorant of other work on the New Testament that would have affected their approach. For example, the great twentieth-century psychologist C. G. Jung, in his book

Answer to Job (Jung, 1954), writes about the book of Revelation in a way that assumes that it was written by the same person who wrote the epistles of St John. However, it is in fact almost universally agreed that different authors were involved. Good psychological interpretation of the Bible should make every effort to be competent in relevant historical-critical material.

A third important guideline is that psychology should not be reductionist in its approach. When psychology gets to work, there is a tendency to assume that whatever is being examined is 'nothing but' a matter of psychology. Though the gospels, on the face of things, testify to the power of God at work in the ministry of Jesus, some psychologists might be tempted to argue that this apparent power can be explained entirely in psychological terms. Such explanations may reduce the degree of depth and richness with which these texts can speak of human life.

Sometimes psychology may indeed provide an adequate explanation of events described in the gospels. However, that is not a necessary consequence of introducing a psychological perspective, but something to be considered and debated in particular cases. More often, it will be helpful to see psychology as representing a complementary perspective; not reducing everything to a matter of psychology, but elucidating the psychological aspect of things more explicitly. The gospels contain a variety of material that is open to psychological interpretation. There are three main categories: the psychology of Jesus himself, the psychology implicit in his teaching, and the psychology of his interaction with people he encountered. We will consider each of these in turn.

The Psychology of Jesus

As has already been noted, there is a long tradition of trying to understand the psychology of Jesus. It has attracted much criticism, because of the sketchy information we have available, and the tendency for rather wild inference to be made by those who have written about Jesus' psychology. However, that does not render the whole enterprise invalid.

It is wise to make a distinction between psychological interpretations of the historical Jesus, and psychological interpretations of Jesus as he is presented in particular gospels. There is clearly a distinction between the two. Everyone would agree that there is much information that would in principle be relevant to the first, but is not recorded in the gospels. Many would also take the view that the Jesus presented in the gospels is of variable authenticity concerning the historical Jesus. Psychological interpretations of either presentation of Jesus should state the source from which such interpretations are derived.

Psychological formulations of the historical Jesus are difficult, but not hopeless. J. W. Miller's book, *Jesus at Thirty* (Miller, 1997) is an interesting example of careful work in this area. For example, the remarks of Jesus in the gospels in which he dissociates himself from his mother and family would be widely regarded as authentic, and have important implications for his mind-set. In contrast, the psychology of Jesus as presented in a particular gospel can bypass questions about the authenticity of the gospel material. Such studies can confine themselves to elucidating what is implicit in different gospel portraits of Jesus (i.e. rendering explicit in psychological terms what is left implicit in the gospels), and avoid the question of whether the gospels present an historically authentic portrait.

It is also possible to use psychology to develop particular views about the person and nature of Jesus, in a way that parallels the use of philosophy for that purpose over the centuries. In some cases, the Christian believer's reverent view of Jesus will, with the aid of psychology, tend to develop into an idealisation of the psychology of Jesus. That is true, for example, of Dominian's psychological study of Jesus from a Catholic perspective (Dominian, 1998). On other occasions, the non-believer's more iconoclastic view of Jesus will tend to develop, in light of a psychological approach, into a critique of Jesus, such as Jay Haley's study of Jesus' power tactics (Haley, 1989). Those who engage in either enterprise will no doubt draw on some of the recorded material about Jesus. However, the enterprise will often be ideologically motivated, albeit illustrated from material in the gospels, rather than arising from a careful and balanced examination of all the relevant material.

There is an interesting divergence among those engaged on the psychological study of Jesus in their attitude to the quest for the historical Jesus. Some see it as allied with the historical quest, and an attempt to get back into the mindset of Jesus of Nazareth, however difficult that might be. Miller's (1997) is an example of that. Others have concluded that the quest for the historical Jesus is a hopeless one, and have distanced psychology from it. Instead they have seen psychology as a way of understanding the Christ of faith, for example, the psychological significance of Christ to those who believe in him. G. Stanley Hall's *Jesus the Christ in the Light of Psychology* (Hall, 1917) explicitly takes this position, and in similar vein Childs (2000) has recently integrated a Jungian understanding of Christ with a very disparaging attitude to the quest for the historical Jesus.

Whatever one thinks about Jesus, his psychology is surely a matter of some interest. However, it may be more than that; the psychology of Jesus may be quite fundamental to our understanding of the exceptional impact that he made. There is a recent trend in New Testament scholarship emphasising Jesus as a spirit-filled Jewish mystic, even that he was in some sense 'possessed' by the Holy Spirit. Such a view can either define the cause of Jesus' distinctive impact as merely a matter of spirit possession, or it can be used to a elucidate, at a human level, the unique way in which Jesus was possessed by, or at 'one' with, the Spirit of God. Either way, psychology will be relevant to our understanding Jesus.

One objection to such an approach is that it is too individualistic, and neglects the socio-political and cultural context in Jesus' time. Certainly that is important, but one can advocate the relevance of psychology to understanding Jesus without going so far as to regard psychology as primary to social aspects. Jesus was massively influenced by his cultural context, and the movement he founded had socio-political implications.

However, that can be fully conceded without drawing the extreme conclusion that the psychology and consciousness of Jesus is a marginal matter of no fundamental importance.

Another objection is that to focus on the psychology of Jesus is to import current preoccupations and assumptions to understanding someone who lived in a very different society, two thousand years ago. Clearly, there are dangers here, and it is good to be aware that some aspects of psychological functioning are culturally dependent (in a way that the natural sciences are not). However, I believe that this objection is often pushed too far. Aspects of human experience and consciousness are made accessible by contemporary psychology in ways that were inaccessible to individuals in Jesus' time. However, it is going too far to claim that there is nothing interesting or important about his psychology for us to access. There is no reason to doubt that psychological functioning was as important then as now. The chief difference is that 2000 years ago there were few tools for conceptualising it; now we have such tools.

This book is divided into three sections. The next two chapters are concerned with the psychology of Jesus himself and how he is portrayed. In the next two chapters we will look at the use of psychology in the study of Jesus. In chapter 2, Justin Meggitt discusses why psychology has not been used more extensively in historical studies of Jesus, and what contribution it is capable of making. Then, in chapter 3, Liz Gulliford turns to modern portrayals of Jesus in the cinema. One of the enduring issues in portraits of Jesus is whether to portray him as human or divine, and how to integrate the two, and that is the issue in cinematic portrayals on which she focuses. The following group of three chapters will be concerned with the message, sayings and encounters of Jesus. The final group of chapters are concerned with what people bring to reading the gospels.

The Encounters and Sayings of Jesus

The psychological interpretation of Jesus' interaction with his contemporaries is more straightforward, and there are two aspects. The first aspect is the personality of the various people he met. As would be expected, they are quite varied, sufficiently so that they form a representative sample of different personality types. Information about them is often rather limited and skeletal, but there is enough for most people to find characters in the gospel with whom they can identify.

Jesus' encounters with people often bring about transformation, and the gospel accounts indicate that this was often achieved in a brief well-judged exchange. Chapter 4 in this book, by Sara Savage, indicates that there are parallels to be drawn between contemporary methods of psychological therapy and the way Jesus related to the people he met. That should not, of course, be taken to imply that he was explicitly following any particular psychological method in his interactions. Rather, the point is that our contemporary knowledge of methods of psychological therapy enables us to identify and make explicit the range of methods used implicitly by Jesus in his various encounters. He does not seem to have used any single, identifiable approach, but to have used different approaches with different people as he saw fit.

The second aspect of interpreting Jesus' interaction with his contemporaries is in his sayings, which also raises different issues. (I prefer 'sayings' to 'teaching' because 'teaching' implies that Jesus was more systematic than he seems to have been; it may also imply that he was a teacher of 'ethics', which is another doubtful assumption.) Much of Jesus' teaching, at least in Matthew, Mark and Luke, is about the 'kingdom'. So, the question of how psychology can help in the elucidation of Jesus' teaching is closely intertwined with the question of what he meant by that.

It would be a mistake, I believe, to argue that the parables of Jesus could be adequately translated into wisdom of a psychological kind. That is not so much because the parables are not psychological, but because they cannot be adequately translated into wisdom of any single kind. They seem to be multi-layered and rich with implications for many different domains of life. That is perhaps why they have captured the popular imagination so effectively and for so long. I believe that the sayings of Jesus have significant psychological importance, but I want to recognise that they have other non-psychological significance as well. It would overlook their uniqueness if we simply reduce them to psychology.

To expend on that point it will be helpful to look briefly, first at the function and form of Jesus' sayings, and then at their content. The form is puzzling and tantalising. Many of the parables lack the clear punchline that you would expect to find in similar stories in other contexts. Jesus is even recorded as explicitly saying that it is not intended that the parables are understood. It seems in their nature to be enigmatic and paradoxical, defying adequate literal explication. That leads on to a suggestion about the function of these sayings; their enigmatic character suggests that Jesus' primary attempt was not to provide a body of 'teaching' but to speak in a way that will jolt people out of their conventional assumptions and move than towards the different order of being that he called his 'kingdom'.

Just as Jesus' sayings seem to defy literal explication, so it also seems impossible to define the 'kingdom' adequately. It seems to point to a new order that is partly religious, partly socio-political, partly existential and psychological. While fully acknowledging the first two strands, I would argue that the existential/psychological aspect of the kingdom is also important. It is significant here that Jesus is recorded as saying that the coming of the kingdom will not be externally detectable because it is 'within' (Luke 17:21). The function of the sayings of Jesus seems to be partly to move people towards an awareness of and a new state of inner being.

Despite the enigmatic character of the sayings, some recurrent threads of psychological meaning do seem to run through them, and I try to elucidate some of these in chapter 5. For example, Jesus repeatedly holds out the promise of radical transformation. He also repeatedly indicates the sacrifices of comfortable living and psychological security that will be needed to move towards it. He seems to be talking about movement from a limited form of adjustment, however satisfactory it may be within its own terms, to something potentially much more fulfilling. There is also a repeated strand of meaning about gathering in what is lost, improbable, and unexpected, suggesting that the 'yonder' to which he encourages people to aspire is a state of wholeness, not just of society, but of the individual person. It is a helpful hermeneutic key to the psychological interpretation of Jesus sayings to see the 'lost' as, amongst other things, a reference to the lost and under-developed or unacknowledged parts of our personalities.

There is much that psychology can contribute to the interpretation of the sayings of Jesus. Erik Erikson (1981), one of the leading neo-Freudian psychologists of the twentieth century, has considered the implications of the sayings of Jesus for the sense of self. Jungian psychology is one approach that has been employed to good effect to elucidate the contribution that Jesus makes to our understanding of the personal journey towards wholeness (e.g. Sanford, 1987). The parables of Jesus also provide a rich opportunity for psychological study, and Ford (1997) has used his background in psychotherapy to focus on how the characters in Jesus' parables are often trapped in mutual misunderstandings. He shows how listening to these parables can liberate those who hear them from similar misunderstandings about their own relationships.

Psychological interpretation can also elucidate the significant motifs that run through the interpretation of the gospels as a whole. For example, Beaumont Stevenson in chapter 6 picks out one particular motif, the breaking of taboos, that recurs at the number of crucial points in the gospel narrative. It is an interesting illustration of how a psychological exegesis explicitly identifies features that can easily be overlooked in material that has become very familiar. Multiple interpretive frameworks are needed to identify all the potentially significant aspects of the gospels, and psychology provides one such interpretive framework.

A more holistic approach to psychological interpretation is to take one particular gospel and offer a commentary on it from a psychological point of view. There are now various commentaries of this kind, but one of the most impressive is that by John Sanford on St John's gospel (Sanford, 1993). In the introduction to his commentary, Sanford makes an interesting historical point about approaches to biblical interpretation. He refers back to the distinction made by several of the Church Fathers between historical and symbolic aspects of biblical interpretation. While much contemporary biblical study is a continuation of the tradition of historical interpretation, Sanford suggests that psychological commentary on the gospels is a continuation of the tradition of symbolic interpretation. There are also psychological studies of John by Anderson (1997), McGann (1988), and Newheart (2001), and studies of Matthew by Kunkel (1987), of Mark by Francis (1997) and McGann (1985), and of Luke by Francis and Atkins (2000).

Reading the Gospels

Reading the gospels is such an encounter between the reader and what is recorded there, and psychology can illuminate different aspects of that interactive process. As we have seen, some psychological studies of the gospels focus on Jesus and what it was like to be him. Studies of the sayings and encounters of Jesus take a more explicitly interactive approach; these are inevitably read with an eye on implications for his interaction with us in the twenty-first century. Psychology also has something useful to say about what different people bring to reading the gospels, and that is the focus of the final group of chapters in this book.

A distinction has often been made between the historical-critical approach to the Bible, which is the main focus of academic biblical studies, and 'readers' reactions' to the Bible. Compared to academic biblical studies, the study of readers' reactions has been much less systematic, and the human sciences have a great deal to contribute here. Different people will react to the gospels in different ways. How they do so will be influenced in part by the preoccupations of the society they belong to. For example, recent interest has been in the fact that the New Testament was written in a culture in which shame was more prominent than guilt, though it has often been read in cultures in which the opposite was true. It is intriguing, in this context, that our present society is perhaps once again becoming more a shame culture than a guilt culture (Watts, 2001).

How people read the New Testament will also be influenced by their personal psychological outlook. In any given society, different people will read the gospels differently, and psychology can help to explain how and why that happens. Some people may react to this idea with concern and urge that people should try to read what is 'really' in the gospels rather than focusing on what they bring to it personally. Some may even argue that people should not allow the message of the gospels to be contaminated by their psychology. There are several responses to be made to that point.

Firstly, no one can read the New Testament, or any other work, in a completely detached, objective way. None of us can stand outside our own tradition, society, and personal history and outlook, and pretend to be people living in a vacuum. We inevitably bring our background to reading any text, and it is better to try to understand that, rather than to pretend it is not happening.

Secondly, if we could successfully pretend to be the reader in a vacuum as we read the New Testament, our reading would probably not 'speak' to us, or have any personal significance for us. The transforming impact of Scripture lies in approaching them on the reader's own terms, coming to them as the person really is, rather than pretending to be detached and purely objective.

Thirdly, understanding why people read the New Testament differently does not necessarily imply an endorsement of these psychological and sociological approaches. Once you understand why you are liable to respond more sympathetically to some things in the New Testament than others, you can make a deliberate effort to notice things you may not be predisposed to see. Understanding how your background and outlook influences your reading of the gospels can actually help you to let the gospels surprise you.

So far, scant attention has been paid to how psychology can help us to understand how different people read the Bible, though Cedric Johnson has written a helpful introduction in *The Psychology of Biblical Interpretation* (Johnson, 1983), and some further discussion is found in chapter 6 of *Soul and Psyche* (Rollins, 1999). To reiterate, psychology is a diverse discipline that encompasses various different approaches, and there are various different aspects of psychology that can help us to understand how people read the gospels differently. In this book we make use of four different domains of psychology in this connection.

Jesse Abell, in chapter 7, draws on frameworks in cognitive psychology to understand how our thought processes affect our interpretation of materials, including texts such as the gospels. He illustrates how these interpretive processes, of which psychology has a good general understanding, are bound to enter into reading the gospels. Next, in chapter 8, James Day approaches the topic from the perspective of developmental psychology, which is broadly defined as a systematic understanding of how people change and develop, cognitively, in their relationships and attachments, and in the stories they construct about themselves. People's psychological development is bound to influence how they read the gospels.

The final two chapters look at the impact of different personality types. Psychology has long tried to bring some order to the diversity of people's personalities by developing various categorisations. It has been a useful approach, though it has always been recognised that most people are not pure examples of any one particular type of personality. In chapter 9 Leslie Francis draws on an approach to personality types derived from Jung, i.e. whether people approach the perception of the world more in terms of sensing or intuition, and whether their judgement processes arise more from thinking or from feeling. Francis has already explored how these different aspects of personality may influence the reading of Mark's gospel (Francis, 1997), Matthew's gospel (Francis and Atkins, 2001) and Luke's gospel (Francis and Atkins, 2000).

In the final chapter, Everett Worthington draws on another approach to personality: the kind of virtues with which people are predominantly concerned. According to Worthington, people tend to approach virtues either from a predisposition towards warmth or a predisposition towards conscientiousness. This divergence is fundamentally important to most people, and they are often less balanced on this divergence than they would like to assume. He goes on to show how these two different approaches to virtues influence our reading of various issues that arise from the gospels such as our understanding of Jesus himself, and how we read particular controversial passages in the gospels.

A book of this kind cannot hope to say everything that might be said about the contribution of psychology to understanding the gospels. However, I hope we have presented enough to indicate the kind of contribution psychology has to offer, to advance the psychological study of the gospels, and to deepen the understanding of the gospels of those who read this book.

2

Justin J. Meggitt

PSYCHOLOGY AND THE HISTORICAL JESUS

Despite a myriad of explorations in fiction and film and its central importance in much Christian popular piety and theological reflection, the psychology of the historical Jesus has not been something that has attracted serious interest from New Testament scholars (McIntyre, 1998, pp. 115–43). Indeed, most do not consider it a legitimate area of study. Such is the strength of feeling on this issue, that those who do venture into this field find themselves and their work consigned to the periphery of scholarly debate and their interest treated as unhistorical and speculative. It is no surprise, for example, that the fullest discussion of the subject in recent decades appeared in the journal *Pastoral Psychology* (2002), not in a journal for the study of the New Testament. As we shall see, this failure is not quite what it appears to be: for all their protestations, most scholars of the historical Jesus do in fact address psychological questions of a kind although they have a long way to go before they begin to produce works that are, psychologically speaking, very illuminating or defensible.

Despite the poverty of writing in this area, some things can be said about the psychology of the historical Jesus. But before we suggest what these might be, it is important that we look at why there has been such a reluctance to undertake this in a formal way. This is a particularly perplexing state of affairs given that (1) Albert Schweitzer, whose publications have greatly influenced the history and preoccupations of scholars examining the historical Jesus, wrote a book directly on this subject (Schweitzer, 1913/1948); (2) the exponential growth in recent years in the number of publications by New Testament scholars that claim to apply social sciences to its interpretation (e.g., Horrell, 1999); and (3) the myriad of confident reconstructions of the life of the historical Jesus that have appeared since the beginning of the so-called 'Third Quest' in the mid-1980s (e.g., Meier, 1999; Sanders, 1985, p. 2; Witherington, 1997). These factors indicate that the situation should have been very different.

The reason for the absence of studies of the psychology of Jesus is more or less self-evident to most New Testament scholars. For the overwhelming majority, psychology and biblical studies just do not mix. Horrell's collection of essays on socioscientific approaches to the Bible contains virtually nothing from a psychological perspective. As Gerd Theissen has observed, 'the rejection of any combination of psychology and exegesis is often presented with … disarming obviousness' (Theissen, 1987, p. 1). However, if we look more closely at the grounds for this common assumption, it becomes clear that objections are rather weak and the actual practices and concerns of a number of scholars who examine the historical Jesus are not as distinct from those of psychology as are often thought.

For many, the problems of using psychology to examine the historical Jesus are of a general kind that could equally be applicable to the study of the psychology of any historical figure. N. T. Wright's (1996) comments are typical of many:

> Such attempts are made from time to time, but have not carried much conviction. After all, as pastors, psychiatrists and psychotherapists know, it is hard enough to

understand the inner workings of someone's psyche (even supposing we could define such a thing with any precision) when they share one's own culture and language and when they co-operate with the process and answer one's questions. How much harder when none of these things are the case. (p. 479)

Few people raising such objections are aware that the strengths and weaknesses of psychohistory have been discussed for some decades, since Eric Erikson's famous study of Luther (Erikson, 1958). Although psychohistory may have fallen out of favour amongst many English-speaking historians, it does not mean that such an approach is self-evidently unreasonable, as Wright and others assume.[1] At the very least scholars such as Wright would benefit from familiarising themselves with current debates around psychohistorical analysis so that their criticisms are somewhat more informed (Szaluta, 1999).

Some people object to the psychological study of the historical Jesus on grounds that are more specific to the figure of Jesus. For a number of scholars there is a theological objection (whether stated or not) stemming from the fear that such a psychological approach will somehow relativise the theological claims of either the text of the Bible or the figure of Jesus himself, through appeal to factors and processes that are all too human (Theissen, 1987, p. 1). Indeed, such an enquiry might reveal 'imperfection, inadequacy, and weakness' (J. R. Beck, 1998). Objections of this kind are not sustainable not least because, if the bases upon which they are made are taken seriously, any study of the *historical* Jesus, not just those that have a concern with psychological questions, would be impossible. However, the most common

---

[1] Psychohistory fell out of favour amongst historians largely because it was too closely associated with Freudian psychoanalysis, and because it emerged just as historians began to turn away from the study of 'great men' and towards the analysis of cultures and populations. For further reading see Burke (1992, pp. 114–18).

complaint specific to the study of the psychology of the historical Jesus is that the sources for our knowledge of Jesus cannot bear the weight of psychological scrutiny. The processes by which the New Testament came to be have led most to doubt the ability of even the earliest records of Jesus to give access to the life of the man himself.[2] Although it is now customary for scholars of the historical Jesus to claim that certain isolated 'facts' of Jesus' life can be determined with a reasonable level of certainty through the application of generally agreed historical criteria (for example, Jesus' baptism by John the Baptist or Jesus' death on a Roman cross), these resulting 'facts' are not treated by historians as of the kind that can be subject to psychological scrutiny without a scholar being accused of engaging in an indefensible level of speculation (see Theissen *et al*. 2002).

Yet, despite their protestations, most New Testament scholars do have something to say about the psychology of the historical Jesus, even if they do not use the language of psychology in articulating it.[3] They often operate with 'common-sense' assumptions about 'human nature' that play a crucial part in various aspects of their reconstructions which often, incidentally, give them a false confidence in their speculations.[4] There is one particular preoccupation of Jesus scholarship on which most New Testament scholars have something to say and in which we

[2] For example, Telford (1998), in his review of Miller (1997), notes two major influences over the information about Jesus as we know it today: (1) the process of selection, emendation and arrangement of the formative Jesus by the early church and for the early church, and (2) the introduction of literary and theological motifs by those who set down the traditions in writing.

[3] What Peter Gay has said of historians in general is also true of New Testament scholars: 'The professional historian has always been a psychologist – an amateur psychologist' (Gay, 1985, p. 6).

[4] For example, E.P. Sanders argues that the historical Jesus could not have sought his own death in order to effect some kind of redemption for others because that 'would make him strange in any century' (despite influential models within Judaism current in his day, such as that evident in 2 Maccabees 7:37–8). According to Sanders, everything else that we know about Jesus makes him a '*reasonable* first-century visionary' (Sanders, 1985, p. 333, emphasis his).

can see them most obviously engaging in amateur psychology of a kind: most historians of the historical Jesus have been happy to speculate, at least to a certain degree, about the motivations and objectives of the historical Jesus, in order to say something, however limited, about his self-understanding (e.g., Dunn, 2003, p. 616). Indeed, Wright criticises those who try to study the psychology of the historical Jesus in the context of his own attempt to justify his extremely bold speculations about Jesus' awareness that he was being the embodiment of God's return to Zion (Wright, 1996, p. 653). To date the question of Jesus' self-understanding often consists of rather arid discussions over whether the historical Jesus could have affirmed a variety of apparently conflicting identities for himself, or what incident in his life might be considered a 'turning point' in his self-aware-ness. The speculations are rather impoverished by this allergy to psychology, and as for all the talk of self-understanding, there has been little reflection on what exactly constitutes the under-standing of selfhood within the context of Jesus' day (for some helpful contextual keys to understanding individuals during Jesus' time, see Malina and Neyrey, 1996).

Some, of course, have ventured to say rather more about the psychology of Jesus, despite the reservations of their colleagues. But, for various reasons, work in this area has yet to achieve a great deal. Much time, for example, has been expended debating whether it is reasonable to classify the historical Jesus as suf-fering from a mental illness of some kind (the focus, for example, of Albert Schweitzer's contribution). This is a legitimate area to examine; after all, it seems likely that the historical Jesus was thought to be mad by some of his contemporaries, including his own family (Mark 3:19b–21). A number also thought him pos-sessed, a designation that indicates that they believed that he exhibited behavioural abnormalities (e.g., Mark 3:22; Matt. 12:24; Luke 11:14; John 8:48). Indeed, John's gospel even records a tradition that Jesus was thought to be suicidal (i.e. John 8:22, although this was not thought to necessarily be an indication of mental illness in this period). Indeed, as I have argued elsewhere, I think it is reasonable to interpret Jesus' treatment by the Romans, so reminiscent of that experienced by his 'insane' near-contemporaries Carabas and Jesus ben Ananias, as providing sufficient grounds for concluding that he was ridiculed and put to death by those who believed him to be out of his senses. But although it seems reasonable to pursue this question, much of the serious work on Jesus' mental health was undertaken early in the twentieth century, and our understanding of mental illness has moved on considerably since then, rendering its results of little value. For example, until relatively recently there seems to have been little awareness that 'madness' as a label is often deployed as part of an attempt to enforce cultural notions of normality. Although, socially speaking, it is reasonable that some of Jesus' contemporaries could well have interpreted his actions and teaching as 'mad' because they seem to have been at variance with many assumptions and practices (albeit within the broad possibilities of first-century Judaism), attempts to engage in a retrospective diagnosis of an organic mental disorder seem peculiarly naïve and crude.

Not much work has been undertaken since this flurry of activity nearly a century ago, despite the enormous shift in our thinking about the nature of psychology. However, the contributions of two scholars do stand out, notably those of John W. Miller and Donald Capps. Although their impact on mainstream biblical studies has been negligible, it is instructive to briefly examine how they have tried to tackle the question of the psychology of the historical Jesus before making a few suggestions of my own.

Of the two, Miller's seems to be the more critically astute work, produced by someone who has a significant reputation within the field of biblical studies. He has argued that the bare outline of Jesus' life, discernible through the application of conventional historical-critical method, can give us sufficient data to allow us to engage in some kind of psychological scrutiny (Miller, 1997, p. 2). Indeed, such information cries out for psychological analysis – particularly of a developmental kind. The outline of Jesus' life before the beginning of his ministry is summarised by Miller (1997) in the following way:

> [the gospels] inform us that he was born into a certain kind of family and place and for many years worked at a certain occupation, and that it was not until he was 'about thirty' that he left home for the Jordan, where he was baptized by a certain type of man and then experienced certain 'temptations' – and that not even then did he launch his own unique mission, but only after the one who had him baptised was arrested. (p. 2)

Miller brings a number of approaches to bear in examining this outline but perhaps the most striking is his use of Daniel Levinson's *The Seasons of a Man's Life* (1978), in which it is argued that there is a definite developmental pattern of specific, age-linked phases that affect the lives of all men, shaping behaviour and governing emotional states and attitudes. For Miller, the age at which Jesus began his ministry (recorded in Luke 3:23 to be 'about thirty') is a crucial period of crisis and transformation for men in general, a period of generative and vocational urgency that explains much about the motivation and form, if not the content, of Jesus' ministry (particularly when other biographical factors are taken into account, such as the loss of his father and his close association with his 'mentor' John the Baptist).

Donald Capps provides a rather more complex and speculative attempt at psychohistory, one which is rather less reticent about applying diagnostic labels to the historical Jesus (Capps, 2000, 2004). In particular, he emphasises the formative significance of Jesus' early experience as a fatherless son with a devalued mother. For Capps this not only caused Jesus to develop into a melancholic depressive with a diffused identity but also drove him to resolve his conflict in one consummate, symbolic action in the temple, in which he both purified his mother and affirmed God as his father.

Both these studies, Capps' more so than Miller's, can be

criticised at the level of exegetical detail and the theoretical assumptions could strike many as rather problematic. For example, given that the average life expectancy of a male Jewish peasant in the Roman Empire at this time was probably in the mid-twenties, it seems odd for Miller to argue for the helpfulness of Levinson's insights about the importance of the age-thirty transition (and which are derived from the study of contemporary North Americans) for understanding Jesus. However, the real difficulty with these accounts of the psychology of the historical Jesus lies in the amount that they rely upon the narrative outline of Jesus' life as presented in the canonical gospels. Historically speaking, it is customary to be extremely suspicious of this. For example, even an event as redolent with potential for making sense of the psychology Jesus as the incident in the temple, something that Capps believes resolved Jesus' conflicted identity, is hard to place in the chronology of Jesus' life with any certainty. Did it, for example, occur at the beginning of Jesus' ministry (as recorded in the gospel of John) or at the end (as recorded in the Synoptic gospels)? Indeed, we should keep in mind the sobering remarks made by Cadbury many years ago, which are as relevant now:

> Probably much that is commonly said about the general purpose of Jesus' life and the specific place in that purpose of detailed incidents is modern superimposition upon a nearly patternless life and upon nearly patternless records of it. (Cadbury, 1937, p. 14)

Even if it does prove possible to distinguish a plausible pattern in the life of Jesus we should also be aware of the likelihood that what has been discovered is not something that can allow us to explore the psychological development of Jesus' self-understanding. It may, for example, only tell us something about the historical Jesus' strategy of progressive self-disclosure (Meyer, 1994, p. 351).

So, to date, the study of the psychology of the historical Jesus

remains in its infancy, still a marginal and problematic under-
taking, with little work of value yet done. But, nonetheless, there
are some things that can be said. Although these are of a rather
general kind, and rather limited in scope, they may provide the
basis for further, more fruitful work. Even those who have been
dismissive of psychological scrutiny of the historical Jesus, such
as Günther Bornkamm who rejected it as 'regressive' and
'doomed to failure' (Bornkamm, 1960, p. 24), have felt that
critical examination of the sources can yield some things about
Jesus' 'personality', an area in which we can make some useful
headway. We can know the kind of person the historical Jesus
was. My optimism in this area should come as no surprise. The
personality of Jesus left a clear impression on the earliest
believers, so much so that it became a basis for some of their
ethical thinking and practice. Paul, for example, could entreat the
Corinthians 'by the meekness and gentleness of Christ' (2 Cor.
10:1) – and assume that the recipients of his letter knew that
Jesus was indeed 'meek' and 'gentle' (whatever those terms
might mean). In particular, the virtues that Jesus exhibited in the
face of death, of both forbearance and submission to God, and
his refusal to return violence with violence, seem to have been
recurring motifs in the pictures of Jesus that emerge from these
traditions and tell us something about the enduring impression
his personality made on his followers:

> Each of us must please our neighbour for the good purpose
> of building up the neighbour. For Christ did not please
> himself; but, as it is written, 'The insults of those who insult
> you have fallen on me.' (Rom. 15:2–3)

> For to this you have been called, because Christ also suffered
> for you, leaving you an example, so that you should follow
> in his steps. 'He committed no sin, and no deceit was found
> in his mouth.' When he was abused, he did not return abuse;
> when he suffered, he did not threaten; but he entrusted
> himself to the one who judges justly. (1 Pet. 2:21–3)

In saying that we can know about the 'personality' of Jesus, I am not arguing that we should make anything much of the direct descriptions of Jesus' emotions in our sources, even though these descriptions can reveal such things as Jesus' anger, compassion or love. The textual traditions behind such details seem too unreliable and it is frankly too hard for a modern reader to make any real sense of what is actually being described (Ehrman, 2005). For example, there is little evidence of early Christian documents being at all concerned with 'introspection', even when they talk about states that seem to have an internal origin (such as compassion) there is no idea of subjective and reflective introspection inherent in the emotion. As Berger puts it, there is, in the understanding of emotions in the New Testament, a lack of the 'subjective middle' between reason and ecstasy (Berger, 2003, p. 130).

Rather, we are on more solid ground if we try to determine what kind of personality is implied in the general praxis and preaching of the historical Jesus, drawing our conclusions from data that is more historically defensible. For example, even if critics disagree over the authenticity of particular parables, it is a striking feature of our sources that the form of teaching most associated with the historical Jesus is one that is open-ended and essentially metaphorical in character. Cannot we deduce something about the character of Jesus from this? What kind of person could choose such a means of conveying their ideas? Just how authoritarian, for example, could the historical Jesus have been? Similarly, Jesus seems to have been thought of by his contemporaries as a successful healer and exorcist of some kind (even if the reasons for his success were a matter of contention), and Jesus seems to have shared such an estimation of himself (e.g., Luke 8:20 and Matt. 12:28). Indeed, as Meier notes: 'Put dramatically, but with not too much exaggeration: if the miracle tradition from Jesus' public ministry were to be rejected *in toto* as unhistorical, so should every other Gospel tradition about him' (Meier, 1994, p. 630). The actual practice of healing seems to have been more visceral than is often assumed and may have involved some kind of sympathetic aspect to it, in which Jesus took on the illnesses he cured (e.g., Isa. 53:4, Matt. 8:14). Cannot we infer from this something about his character? Similarly, it seems that Jesus' ministry was characterised by what Crossan (1991, p. 261) has termed 'open commensality', a radical form of social praxis that disturbed social expectations and conventions that Jesus persisted with despite attracting ridicule. Surely such behaviour must allow us to infer something about his psychology? Like- wise, surely we can deduce something from the fact that Jesus seems to have believed that his followers would value him above their families and even their own lives as he asked them to fol- low him (e.g., Mark 8:34–7)? Cannot we legitimately assume something from the intensely eschatological character of his preaching? Of course, the terminology we use to describe Jesus' personality is not self-evident and we will need to pay close attention to cross-cultural taxonomies of personality developed elsewhere to produce anything useful from such a line of enquiry (see, for example, Berry *et al.* 1992, pp. 99–163) but I believe it is evident, from the myriad of data that we have just touched upon, that we can say something.

So, after a rather extended and pessimistic description of the state of scholarship on the question of the psychology of the historical Jesus, I have tried to finish on a positive, if rather undeveloped note. Others, I am sure, can think of more pro- ductive areas to examine. For example, despite the problems with Miller and Capps, it seems legitimate to try to saying something developmental about Jesus' psychology – after all, the early Christians believed that 'he learned obedience through what he suffered' (Heb. 5:8). If more New Testament scholars could be encouraged to recognise that they are already, to some extent, engaged in psychological analysis of the historical Jesus, and that they are, as a matter of course, examining data of real potential psychological significance, much could be gained. The present state of affairs has gone on too long.

3

Liz Gulliford

FULLY HUMAN, FULLY DIVINE? THE CINEMATIC PORTRAYAL OF CHRIST

In this chapter I can do no more than skim the surface of the portrayal of Christ in cinema. What I would like to do is consider some general questions about the relationship between culture and theology and the problems of depicting Christ on the silver screen. I would then like to pose a more specific question about Christ's human psychology, and the emphasis this theme receives in three Christ films: *Jesus Christ Superstar* (Jewison, 1973), *The Last Temptation of Christ* (Scorsese, 1988), and *The Passion of the Christ* (Gibson, 2004). I hope that this necessarily selective review will provide the opportunity to examine the 'two natures' Christology in relation to cinema, and will help us to judge whether the Jesus we encounter there is truly fully human and fully divine.

Spellbound: The Captivating Power of Film

Film has undeniably exerted a huge impact on world culture since its advent at the turn of the twentieth century. There are films that offer a means of escape from the routine events of life in the form of fantasy. On the other hand, there are also films that confront us with the gritty reality of our existence. Either way, for the duration of a film, the audience is exposed to a particular narrative about the way things are, or about the way they could be. As such, film could be said to be 'preaching' to us in parable, or offering us a mythical picture of a transformed world, as noted by David John Graham (1997, p. 39).

This immersion in the narrative can be totally absorbing. The large screen and dramatic surround-sound score narrow our attention in such a way that few, if any, other media can achieve. When we sit in the dark cinema, we prepare to give ourselves over completely for a few hours to the power that it can have over us: a power that is potentially transforming.

Some of the more technical aspects of cinema help to engage us more fully. Clever use of colour can suggest a particular mood; black and white can be used to convey nostalgia but also starkness, even horror. Frames can be frozen, speeded up or shown in slow motion to capture particular moods and secure our emotional investment. Camera angles can also be used to good effect: a close-up lays bare the emotions a character is experiencing, facilitating empathy (or its opposite) with that individual. Panoramas may serve other functions apart from the obvious role of 'locating' the film. For example, after a relatively lengthy focus on a character, the panorama may be used to 'pull away' before focusing on another character (a form of emotional disengagement). Camera angles also suggest 'objective' and 'subjective' perspectives on the unfolding drama: we may be privileged to see through the eyes of victim and perpetrator; man and woman; adult and child.

Films also make use of 'flashbacks', which serve a variety of functions. A flashback can, on the one hand, provide the viewer with missing information about a period relevant to the story that happened long ago. On the other hand, it invites us into the mind of the character by presenting us with emotionally salient memories. We will see later how this use of the flashback is used to very good effect in *The Passion of the Christ*. In short, cinematic techniques can control the type and amount of visual and audio stimuli in order to convey the film's message most effectively (for a good, short summary and technical aspects of cinema see Browne, 1997).

Brief Encounter: Engaging with Theology

Film can contribute to the making of theology by posing questions that bear on such things as the nature of sacrifice and forgiveness, what it means to be human, our purpose and destiny, and personal and collective transformation. All this can happen in films that have no obvious religious subject matter. The films to which we are about to turn, however, do have explicit religious content, and have been hugely significant in informing the views people commonly hold about the person of Christ. As Telford writes in 'Jesus Christ movie star: The depiction of Jesus in the cinema' in *Explorations in Theology and Film*, 'The Christ film is arguably the most significant medium through which popular culture this century has absorbed its knowledge of the Gospel story and formed its impression of Christianity's founder' (Telford, 1997, pp. 121–2).

Film thus appears to hold a key place in presenting the gospel to society, and in varying measure, theological interpretations of the gospel. It could perhaps be argued that film now occupies the place theologically that hymns did in Wesley's time. Is this going too far? Vast numbers of people flocked to hear Wesley's sermons and there was much religious enthusiasm as a result. That said, a large number of Christ films have been box-office successes; they too have drawn supportive and criticising crowds. If film does have this influential role it can offer a vivid means of challenging entrenched representations of religion. Film is literally at the 'cutting edge' of enlivening theology and challenging the world to engage with the gospel message.

The Bible has inspired film-making since the early days of cinema. According to Telford (1997), no fewer than thirty-nine versions of the life of Christ had been filmed before Cecil B. de

Mille's *King of Kings* in 1927. De Mille claimed that he sought to show the 'true humanity' of the biblical characters he portrayed; this however seems to have been true only of the relatively minor roles but not of Christ himself. The actor who played Jesus was kept apart from the rest of the cast to ensure that he maintained a kind of 'rarefied' demeanour.

In Britain the very depiction of Christ in film was banned following the founding of the British Board of Film Censors in 1912, and was lifted only after the second world war. In those days, it seems, the primacy of Christ's divinity predominated to such an extent that even attempting to represent his humanity (in acting) was considered blasphemous.

This Beautiful Mind: The Full Humanity of Christ

The Two Natures Christology holds that the person of Christ is fully human and fully divine. Being fully human entails having a human mind. Our 'humanity' is not simply our physical bodies; we are subject to human emotions, human desires and the limitations of human reason. This presents something of a conundrum: if Jesus has this human psychology, how does it cohere with his also being in possession of a divine, completely compassionate and omniscient mind?

The problem posed by the idea of the coexistence of human and divine in the one person of Christ has often been 'resolved' by the notion that the human component is the body, whilst the divine is the animating spirit. But this falls into a heresy known as Apollinarianism, which was finally condemned at the First Council of Constantinople in AD 381. At the time when Apollinaris, Bishop of Laodicea, Syria was writing, the Platonic tripartite view of man's nature predominated. Man was conceived in a three-level fashion as consisting of body, 'sensitive soul' (which equates to a kind of sensory, non-cognitive perception) and rational soul (the 'mind' as we would understand it today). Apollinaris believed that the presence of this rational soul resulted in an intractable dualism and so he taught that the

Logos (divine nature in Christ) took the place of this rational human soul (mind).

Apollinaris' uneasiness concerning the 'rational human soul' went even further than this logical conundrum. Since free will pertains to the rational soul, and where there is free will, there is sin (he believed), it followed that if Jesus were in possession of this human mind he would not only be compromised by two sources of rationality, but he would also be, along with the rest of humanity, a sinner.

The central issue in the condemnation of Apollinaris revolved around soteriology. If Jesus did not possess a human mind, then a human mind could not be redeemed. Jesus must be everything that is human to redeem and transform humanity, and so the slogan 'what is not assumed cannot be healed' came to be associated with repudiating the heresy. This was not quite the end of the story, however, and Apollinarianism persisted into at least the fifth century at which point its adherents merged with the monophysites. This latter group believed, quite simply, that Christ had only one, that is, divine nature. Another relevant doctrinal spat (monothelitism) suggested that Jesus experienced human emotions, but did not possess a human will. This omission of the conative aspect of Jesus' psychology makes a mockery of the temptation in the wilderness and of Gethsemane.

Ultimately, we may find such heretical solutions attractive because they resolve disturbing and dissonant chords. How could Jesus have simultaneously possessed a human mind that was not totally overshadowed by a divine mind? But, at the last, these heretical positions are unsatisfactory and we are bound to admit the alternative logic, that Jesus could not have redeemed human minds had he not been in possession of such a 'rational soul' himself'. For Jesus to be fully human he must be in possession of this human psyche, regardless of how problematic the Chalcedonian Definition feels to us: 'our Lord Jesus Christ to be one and the same Son, perfect in divinity and humanity, truly God and truly human, with a rational soul and a body' (Council of Chalcedon, 451; cited in McGrath, 1995, p. 148).

The question that concerns us here is how do cinematic portrayals of Christ deal with this issue? Do we see concerted attempts to portray this human side, more specifically this human mind in film? As I mentioned briefly, the tendency in the early Hollywood epics was rather to ignore the humanity of Christ and slink into a fairly Apollinarian position. This tendency has changed recently with more deliberate attempts to portray Christ's human emotions, desires and will, though the extent to which this is possible depends on the director's willingness to go beyond the biblical accounts in order to emphasise this humanity which is so central to Christian theology.

I shall now discuss the human and divine aspects of Christ in each of the chosen films. In some cases this humanity subsumes both the physical and the psychological, but since these are intertwined and I do not wish to draw a dualistic wedge between them, I include them both in the 'human' category, though I shall attempt to focus on the psychological import. We begin with the upbeat musical *Jesus Christ Superstar*. The opening scene depicts a busload of actors arriving on location in Israel preparing to portray the events of the Passion in dance and song. By showing the cast arriving on set, writer/director Norman Jewison explicitly points out that what is about to unfold is an interpretation of the gospel in the form of a rock and roll musical.

Jesus Christ Superstar

At the beginning of the film Judas raises the question of Jesus' messianic consciousness (whether Jesus knew he was the Messiah). A desperately worried Judas dashes back and forth in front of the camera, imploring us to share in his concern about the legend growing up around Jesus. In the opening song, 'Heaven on their minds', Judas asks himself, and by implication the audience, whether Jesus truly believes he is the anointed one:

> 'You've started to believe the things they say of you,
> you surely don't believe this talk of God is true?'

'I remember when this whole thing began
No talk of God then; we called you a man.'

The audience is being asked to consider whether Jesus 'super-
naturally' knows he is the Messiah, or is instead a regular guy on
whom this most holy honour is being conferred. This thread
reaches its climax later in the film with the title song 'Jesus
Christ, Superstar', where the question of Jesus knowing his
divinity is more clearly posed:

'Jesus Christ, Superstar
Do you think you're who they say you are?'

To answer that question in the affirmative can only mean that the
divine Logos dwells in Christ. The issue is raised early in the
film. It is put into the mouth of a sceptical Judas, but it challenges
the audience to consider the human Jesus of history and the
divine Christ of faith. How might the human mind of Christ
have reacted to the divine omniscience that assured him of his
mission as Messiah? In the film, Jesus does not give an explicit
answer to the question: 'Do you think you're who they say you
are?' The question is presented as something for viewers to
ponder, but the overriding impression is that Jesus himself is not
in any doubt about his role. Jesus' quiet and dignified divinity is
emphasised and made apparent in his anointing by Mary Magdalene. Jesus accepts the anointing in a matter-of-fact way: he
seems comfortable with all that the anointing symbolises about
who he is.

Having mentioned Mary Magdalene, the film goes beyond the
gospel accounts to hint at a relationship between Mary and Jesus.
In other respects the film is largely very faithful to the gospels.
Perhaps the purpose of this addition is to portray another
dimension of Jesus' humanity: his sexual desires and drives.
If that is the intention, however, it seems rather weak. Mary
proclaims Jesus' humanity with the words 'He's a man, he's just
a man', but this is sung while Jesus is sleeping and thus

incapable of offering his own contributions. All we see of the hinted relationship is Mary's (potentially unrequited) love, and this cannot be said to challenge our views about Jesus' sexuality to any significant degree. Mary may not 'know how to love him', but we can only guess at whether Jesus himself shares these passionate feelings.

Jesus is presented as one who is comfortable with being glorified. In 'Christ you know I love you', Jesus accepts praise from followers singing, 'I believe in you and God so tell me that I'm saved'. The people clearly do not understand what power and glory will ultimately mean for Jesus, but Jesus seems to be at ease with being honoured as saviour.

Jesus' omniscience is underscored: he clearly knows what lies in store for him. Mary Magdalene comments at the arrest: 'It's what he told us he would do ... I wonder how he knew?' Thus the notion of Jesus' messianic consciousness is a recurrent motif in the film. It points the viewer to the conclusion that there was very definitely a divine and omniscient mind in Christ. But how, on the other hand, is the humanity of Christ handled? Do we see glimpses of psychological weakness, in addition to the presentation of 'weak flesh'?

The clearest indication of a human mind is perhaps, not surprisingly, encountered in Gethsemane where, in the canonical gospels themselves, Jesus desires to be spared the cup of suffering. The song elaborates on the psychological themes of fear, suffering and anger, and there is a very definite pitting of Jesus' human will against God's redemptive purposes:

> 'Why should I die?'
> 'What you started...I didn't start it.'

Jesus laments in frustration that he has 'worked for three years, seems like thirty, seems like ninety'. We are invited to consider that Jesus' forbearance is nearly exhausted. The song ends with a clear reference to Christ's human mind in a rather ambiguous giving of himself to God's higher purposes:

'Your will is hard, but you hold every card.'
'Take me now before I change my mind.'

In contrast to some of the earliest Christ films, few miracles are portrayed in *Jesus Christ Superstar*. When a group healing is portrayed, people come from far and wide to touch Jesus, but rather than this representing an opportunity to demonstrate the wonder of these acts, we are instead presented with a tired, even irritable, Christ. The unmistakable signs of exhaustion are clear to see on his face. This alerts us to the fact that there were limits as to how far Jesus could go in these healings, which are depicted as literally 'taking it out of him'.

Although the cleansing of the temple is often invoked as an example of how Christ 'got angry' and experienced human emotion, the majestic way the act is carried out does not suggest his anger was out of control or inappropriate. Besides, it could plausibly be argued that what we see in the temple cleansing is not simply human anger but also, perhaps even predominantly, divine wrath. I am not, therefore, convinced that this episode tells us much about the human emotion of Christ, though this is not a criticism of the film but of the way that passage is often understood. On the cross all of the sayings, except the most masterful Johannine 'It is accomplished' are used, suggesting that the intention may have been to play down Christ's divinity at the moment of ultimate sacrifice.

One thing I find particularly interesting about this film is that nowhere in it does 'the Lord of the dance' actually dance! This is surely noteworthy in a musical where the rest of the cast engages in some high-octane movements. One would imagine that the reason for this is to create an aura of peace and majesty around Jesus, but this would seem to reinforce, to some extent, the older 'rarefied' portrayals of Jesus in early cinema. There is also no attempt to present any sense of conflict between the human mind and the divine Logos until the crisis of Gethsemane. As we have seen, the humanity of Christ, and in particular some psychological consideration of Christ's humanity, is not entirely lacking.

In tackling this theologically, however, there is very little going beyond the biblical material and something of a reticence to really 'put Jesus' whole self in'.

The Last Temptation of Christ

In comparison to the previous film, this film shows a more concerted effort to present (alongside the divine nature of Christ) a human nature in Jesus, in all its weaknesses and frailty. The film, directed by Martin Scorsese in 1988, is based on the book titled *O Teleutaios Peirasmos* (translated as *The Last Temptation*) by Greek writer Nikos Kazantzakis (first published in 1951; translation into English 1998). Its opening credits explain that the film is not based entirely on the gospels but 'on the eternal spiritual conflict between the Spirit and the Flesh'. Rather than offering us a 'life of Christ', the film instead brings into sharp theological focus the problems posed by the Two Natures Christology. It is well known, however, that in going beyond the gospels (even in the pursuit of theological interests) the film sparked a good deal of controversy.

The plot follows the gospels fairly closely up to the crucifixion but as Jesus is dying on the cross, he fantasises about the comforts of family life and is tempted for one last time not to give himself up in the crucifixion – his last temptation. Although this is the most major departure from the gospel accounts, throughout the film we are presented with a different sort of Jesus from what we have to come to regard as the norm. Instead of a serene and assured Jesus we encounter a man who has an ambiguous attitude towards his calling and is a self-confessed coward.

In the opening scene we encounter a tortured Jesus, a carpenter making crosses for the Romans 'so that God will hate him.' Jesus is weary of God's pursuit but knows that God will abide with him: 'You can't cast out God, can you?' It becomes apparent that Jesus' human psyche resists the privileged knowledge to which he has access: 'You think it is a blessing to know what God wants?' The overwhelming impression is one of conflict and inner struggle, a theme that reaches its culmination on the cross. Jesus emphasises his weaknesses, describing himself to Judas as a hypocrite and a coward who is afraid of everything. Shortly afterwards the question put to those bent on stoning Mary Magdalene: 'Which of you has never sinned?' is all the more poignant because they have recently heard Jesus speak of his own sins with such conviction. However, in reflecting on this incident later it is clear that Jesus' divine spirit is also directing his actions and making him super-humanly compassionate: 'I wanted to kill Magdalene's torturers. I open my mouth and love comes out. I don't understand.' This represents a clear statement of the paradox of the human and divine minds coexisting in the person of Christ. Here that paradox is put into the mouth of Christ himself. Even he cannot comprehend it.

In the wilderness Jesus is tempted by the prospect of his leading a normal family life, a temptation later relived on the cross in the 'last temptation'. In the gospel accounts the temptation is an assertion of Christ's humanity and his struggle to resist the impulse towards earthly comforts, power and dominion. However, in this film we are especially aware of how difficult a struggle this is, having also witnessed how violently Jesus resisted his calling.

Interestingly, in this film Jesus joins the dance at the wedding in Cana. This might seem a small detail but it speaks of embodiment and demonstrates how far portrayals of Christ have come in recognising Jesus Christ as an embodied being. But as this human side, both body and soul, is presented we also come face to face with a Jesus who can perform the most profound miracle. While *Jesus Christ Superstar* depicted Jesus in mass healings, *The Last Temptation* opts to present us with one huge miracle demonstrating Jesus' ultimate power: the raising of Lazarus from the dead. And when Jesus is challenged in the temple about whether God has changed his mind about the old law, Jesus responds with, 'God and I are one'.

This affirmation of oneness with God stands at odds with Jesus' later comments to Judas about God's plan, where the human mind of Christ appears to comment on divine redemptive purpose: 'Love, axe, death – every day a different plan'. Interestingly, this plan is portrayed as involving the agency of both Jesus and Judas: 'We're bringing God and man together. You have to kill me. Turn me in. God gave me the easier job – be crucified.' The events of Gethsemane closely follow the gospels with some small elaborations: 'You opened the Red Sea for Moses .... Do I have to die?' The crucifixion also follows the gospels with several additional utterances to underscore Jesus' sense of alienation from God. As Jesus is being nailed to the cross he cries: 'Stay with me.... Don't leave me'. We are left in no doubt as to Christ's frailty and utter sense of abandonment. The Lucan saying, 'Father forgive them' is included, before the Matthean and Markan saying, 'My God, my God, why have you forsaken me?' This ushers in the part of the film that caused most controversy: the fantasy on the cross.

Although we have already seen some of the ways in which this film might have courted controversy (such as its portrayal of a Christ who regarded his calling ambiguously), by far the most upset came from a part of the film which departed significantly from the gospels to present a Christ wrestling with one final temptation. The 'last temptation' describes a fantasy which Jesus experiences in his last hours on the cross. In the heat and agony of the execution it is very likely that those who had been crucified would have experienced delirium and hallucinations. In this departure from the gospels, Jesus' 'guardian angel' appears and tells Jesus that he does not have to be sacrificed: he is not the Messiah. The 'angel' shows Jesus the life he would have were he not to 'drink the cup': Jesus marries Mary Magdalene, who later dies bearing his child. He remarries Mary, sister of Lazarus and enjoys family life.

In this fantasy Jesus also encounters the apostle Paul who is preaching about the resurrected Jesus. He calls Paul a liar: 'I'm a man like everyone. God saved me.' Paul retorts, 'This people's only hope is in the resurrected Jesus. I'll crucify you. I'll resurrect you. People need God. My Jesus is more important and

powerful'. Although the emphasis of the fantasy is on the ultimate temptation that might have wrested Jesus from the cross
(the comforts of family life), the inclusion of the meeting with
Paul seems to serve a more theological and intellectual function.
Once more the viewer is being summoned to consider the relationship between the Jesus of history and the Christ of faith. In
this instance the necessity for the creation of myth is explicitly
articulated: 'I'll crucify you. I'll resurrect you. People need God.'
It is not difficult to see why this frankly functionalistic portrayal
of Paul adds fuel to the flames of controversy. However, as it is
part of the fantasy, it simply poses a question about the role the
apostles had in proclaiming the significance of Jesus Christ. In
much the same way, the fantasy of the 'last temptation' exhorts
us to consider that the struggle with Jesus' human emotions,
desires and will was not yet over even at Golgotha, and continued even as he was dying.

There is a third dimension to the fantasy where Jerusalem is on
fire and an elderly Jesus lies dying. He is visited by Judas who
says, 'I betrayed you because I loved you. Your place was on the
cross. You ran away.' In effect Jesus' fantasy presents him as a
coward who could not go through with his calling to die on the
cross. In the fantasy it is Judas who exposes the 'guardian angel'
for what she is: Satan. This, then, is the 'opportune time' of
which Satan had warned Jesus after the tempting in the wilderness. Jesus rises above this 'last temptation' and comes to
himself lamenting his sin: I'm a selfish and unfaithful son. Can
you forgive me? Take me back?'

As the realisation dawns that Jesus has been tempted but has
risen victorious over sin, the fantasy ends and we return to the
cross. Jesus has fulfilled his calling and fittingly the film ends
with the Johannine saying, 'It is accomplished'. Thus 'the last
temptation' itself is extra-biblical, although the film ends in an
orthodox fashion. Jesus fulfils his vocation in spite of the great
struggle we have witnessed throughout the film between his
human emotions, thinking and will and the redemptive purpose
of the divine logos.

The Passion of the Christ

Although the scourging and crucifixion scenes of all Christ films are painful to watch, by far the most violent Christ film yet made is *The Passion of the Christ* released at Easter 2004 and directed by Mel Gibson. As its title suggests, the film opens in Gethsemane and portrays the events of Jesus' arrest, trial, scourging and crucifixion. The film's focus on the Passion inevitably means that there is already a strong emphasis on the humanity of Christ: his anxiety and fear in the garden, his horrendous suffering, and his painful death on the cross. As Jesus prays fervently in Gethsemane, a snake slithers across his path. There is a suggestion here of the second Adam: the serpent points to the humanity of Jesus and the temptation he has to resist.

Flashbacks are used to great effect in this film and appear to serve a dual function. They provide missing pieces of the story to viewers who may not be familiar with the events that have preceded the Passion, and they invite us invite us into Jesus' inner life as we see the past through his eyes; what he was remembering, attending to and meditating upon as he drew closer to Golgotha.

The Passion of the Christ is much more of an 'action film' than any of the other films discussed here. In many scenes there is little dialogue, and it is a much less intellectual film than *The Last Temptation*. Some material in the film, the scourging for example, relies on historical accounts of the manner in which a scourging was perpetrated: it is an almost unwatchable scene of the most unspeakable cruelty. Its intention, I would argue, is to impress upon a generation of movie-goers accustomed to the action-genre and familiar with bloody violence, that the death Christ endured on the cross was of the most horrific kind, and that sanitised portrayals of this death have misrepresented, even trivialised, the agony of Jesus' last hours. The film, as its title suggests, is not concerned so much with intellectual, theological questions, so much as with the suffering of Jesus' spirit, mind and body.

The film begins in Gethsemane. Jesus, alone, shows all the normal signs of fear. He sweats and shivers, and prays to God asking him to 'rise up' and 'defend him'. This portrayal of Christ begins with a biblical passage that truly depicts a man who is 'sorrowful unto death'. After Jesus has been arrested he sees a nail which gives rise to a flashback of his time as a carpenter. In this extra-biblical flashback, Jesus is making a table, Mary asks him if he is hungry and they joke together. The flashback works on three levels: first, it provides the naïve viewer with some 'back story' (that Jesus had a fairly normal life as a carpenter). Second, it underscores Jesus' earthliness and humanity, as a man who enjoyed family, banter and a good meal. Third, the nail points not only to the past but also to the future, towards his crucifixion. It could be argued that on this third level, the nail penetrates Jesus' messianic consciousness, and serves as a powerful stimulus that ignites the associations of both the human and divine minds of Christ; one pointing forward, the other going back.

In the midst of the arrest, Jesus heals one of the arresting soldier's ears, an incident recorded in Luke's gospel (Luke 22:50–51). None of the other Christ films discussed here include this detail. It is an act of compassion surely beyond what is humanly possible at such a time, and one that demonstrates Jesus' supernatural healing power. There is then, a clear presentation of Christ's divinity alongside the portrayal of his humanity.

There is no doubt that the torture of the scourging is of the most horrific kind and that Jesus' pain is real. The torturing soldier's sandal is a cue for another flashback: 'If the world hates you remember that it hated me first' (John 15:18). We are again invited, via the flashback, to imagine what Jesus might have been thinking as he endured the brutality and humiliation of the scourging. As Jesus is led out to be crucified, awkward lurching camera angles and further flashbacks are used to further enable us to take up Jesus' perspective as he carries the cross to Golgotha.

When Jesus falls with the weight of the cross, Mary's flashback recalls her distress at seeing him falling as a child. Jesus is flesh of Mary's flesh, and she suffers to see him in pain now just as she did when he was small. As they near Golgotha Jesus recalls his own saying: 'If you love those who love you, what reward do you have?' (Matt. 5:46; see also Luke: 6:32) There is a sense of Jesus striving to recall this maxim and to live (and die) by it in his agony. This determination continues with Jesus calling to mind the Last Supper and sayings from the farewell discourses as the crucifixion takes place.

Unlike the other films, there is an explicit resurrection appearance as Christ is shown getting up from the tomb. Although this highlights Christ's divinity and triumph over death, the biblical reference to the scars of the nails on Jesus' hands is retained, bearing witness to the suffering his human frame endured.

The Passion of the Christ was regarded by many as unnecessarily violent. I do not, however, share the view that it was a 'glorification of violence' or that the cruelty it depicted was merely gratuitous. The film aims to depict precisely the kind of suffering the scourging would have entailed, and in so doing it demonstrates the dehumanisation of torture and the brutality Christ endured. It is a horrific scene, but one that compellingly depicts Christ's compassionate endurance unto death. Although the depiction of the struggle between the human and divine minds and wills is less direct, less sustained and less elaborated than in *The Last Temptation of Christ*, I would argue that it is nonetheless present, and quite cleverly and subtly portrayed.

Concluding Remarks

The way that Christ has been portrayed in film has changed considerably since the beginning of cinema. At first, representing Christ physically was altogether banned. Once this stumbling block had been negotiated, the scandal really inhered not so much in Christ's physicality – the 'flesh' had never really been an issue as the Apollinarian controversy revealed – but in how to portray the paradox of human and divine minds coexisting in the person of Christ. Could Christ be allowed to exhibit human emotions, desires, and a will that occasionally clashed with the divine redemptive purpose of the Logos? Would Jesus be allowed to demonstrate a degree of ambiguity about his calling, and suggest that it was not, perhaps, a blessing to know what God wants? Was Jesus forever to go meekly and stoically to the cross, apparently virtually devoid of human emotion, or could he make his tortuous way to Golgotha, striving to live and die by his own teachings, and struggling with temptation unto his last breath?

This paradox is nothing new. We encounter it in the gospels and in the history of theology. Cinema, however, offers a powerful means of drawing out and commenting on the paradox, reaching beyond the gospels themselves to elucidate its implications to a wide audience. More recent cinematic portrayals of Christ have emphasised the import of Jesus' human mind, redressing the balance of the Hollywood epic. But, ultimately and importantly, altering this balance is all one can attempt: the paradox cannot logically be resolved. The person of Christ is fully human and fully divine: 'perfect in divinity and humanity, truly God and truly human, consisting of a rational soul and a body, being of one substance with the Father in relation to his divinity, and being of one substance with us in relation to his humanity' (Council of Chalcedon, 451; cited in McGrath, 1995, p. 148).

4

Sara Savage

HEALING ENCOUNTERS

Psychological Perspectives on Jesus' Healing

Writers of the gospels did not flinch from recording counter-cultural and unflattering details. Surprising elements in Jesus' encounters with others must have burned themselves upon collective memory. These 'unedited' details have a ring of truth, and through them, an incisive psychological understanding is revealed. Not that we claim that the gospels were written as a psychological account in the modern sense of the word; rather they were carefully constructed to convey a theology concerning the person of Christ. Even so, these startling details, when unpacked, reveal a depth of insight and compassion befitting the most transformational of psychotherapeutic encounters. In this chapter, we will use various psychological perspectives to enable a fresh look at three healing encounters: two from the gospel of John and one from the gospel of Luke. We will be using these diverse psychological theories as lenses through which to contemplate these gospel narratives.

To explore the human significance of the content of Jesus' interactions, we will touch upon theories of human need from psychoanalytic, cognitive and behaviourist traditions. Aspects of these theories will be described in relation to the three gospel accounts. These psychological traditions are rooted in different conceptions of human nature, employ different methods of investigation (with varying degrees of empirical substantiation), and assume different values. We need not worry about these disagreements here; writers of the four gospels also saw things from different points of view. We will simply use these contrasting psychological theories as different angles from which to consider the richness of human experience recorded in these gospel accounts.

To examine the deeper structure of Jesus' interactions with others, a further layer of interpretation will be added to the various theories used. Healing encounters in the gospels take place in the context of a relationship (between the healer and person needing healing), and often explicitly involve the healing of the social relationships within that particular context. What kind of relationship does Jesus enact? What are his interpersonal 'rules of engagement'? To help unveil structural regularities in Jesus interpersonal behaviour, we draw on an interactional strategy modelled by a computer programme called Tit for Tat (Axelrod, 1984).

It may seem strange to pair a strategy used in economics and evolutionary psychology with this unrivalled charismatic healer from the first century! We hope that the fit will become evident as the chapter unfolds, and here we offer some explanation. The computer programme Tit for Tat tests the effects of highly simplified interactions between itself and other players. All players, over any number of iterations, can choose one of two ways to interact: to cooperate or to defect. Tit for Tat's first player's initial move is always to cooperate. Yet it also responds effectively to 'defectors' (other players who will not cooperate or, in human terms, who fail to interact in a pro-social manner). Tit for Tat does precisely what the preceding player has done on the previous move; cooperative moves are met with cooperation, defection is met with defection.

In comparison with other strategies such as All Defect (in

which the player competes at all times with or defects at all times against others) or All Cooperation (in which the player cooperates at all times towards all others), Axelrod's Tit for Tat won two national tournaments and was clearly the most effective. Broadly speaking, Tit for Tat-like strategies are the best way of responding to the potential for the cooperation *and* defection of others. In computer simulations, this kind of strategy can 'invade' and eventually overcome a population of defectors. This remarkable discovery has contributed towards acceptance among evolutionists that natural selection, normally thought of as invariably aggressive and selfish, can select for 'pro-social' Tit for Tat-like strategies that cooperate with cooperation but defect against defection.

What insight can this strategy afford to the healing encounters of Jesus? We suggest that this strategy can work as an interpretive lens that contrasts with some common assumptions of Jesus' healing ministry. Jesus as healer has often been depicted as a psychological docetist: his eyes rolled heavenward, disengaged from the messiness of human interaction, invariably acting as a one-way street of free-floating goodness – All Cooperation. By viewing the structural regularities in Jesus' interpersonal style through the lens of the Tit for Tat strategy, we see a more interesting and fuller humanity, and a more demanding interpersonal style that cannot hide behind futile attempts at unsustainable behaviour. (For who among us can maintain a free-floating one-way street of goodness?)

Four features of Tit for Tat

Tit for Tat is inevitably too simple to account for the complexities of human interpersonal behaviour. However, if we concentrate here on the broad structure of interactions, we find an interesting 'fit' with the four features of Tit for Tat: generosity, robustness, forgiveness and clarity (Badcock, 2000).

Generosity

Tit for Tat's first move is always generous, and welcomes cooperation. Jesus invites his followers and promises they will be a part of something extraordinary: ' "Come, follow me," Jesus said, "and I will make you fishers of men." ' (Mark 1:17, NIV).

Robustness

Tit for Tat's response to another's defection is to defect immediately so that it cannot be exploited beyond one defection. Here we take a bit of artistic license in applying Tit for Tat: there is no evidence of Jesus retaliating or paying back in a vindictive spirit. Yet he does meet defections with an immediate boundary or rebuttal, one that seeks to enlighten his 'opponent' in order to afford him or her the freedom to choose another way. It is in this sense that his interactions are 'robust', and henceforth we rename the strategy Enlightened Tit for Tat when applied to Jesus' interactions.

Forgiveness

Tit for Tat returns to cooperation as soon as the other player does so. By immediately rewarding cooperation, mutual cooperation is encouraged. We see Jesus readily restoring the repentant with a forgiveness that lavishes the blessings of restoration.

Clarity

The simplicity and transparency of the Tit for Tat strategy means that opponents 'learn the rules' very quickly, and thus can learn to respond appropriately.

Resourced thus with these psychological theories with which we refract both content and structure of Jesus' interpersonal behaviour, we now turn to three healing encounters.

Jesus and a Woman of Samaria: John 4:3b—30

[Jesus] left Judea and started back to Galilee. But he had to go through Samaria. So he came to a Samaritan city called

Sychar, near the plot of ground that Jacob had given to his son Joseph. Jacob's well was there, and Jesus, tired out by his journey, was sitting by the well. It was about noon. A Samaritan woman came to draw water, and Jesus said to her, 'Give me a drink'. (His disciples had gone to the city to buy food.) The Samaritan woman said to him, 'How is it that you, a Jew, ask a drink of me, a woman of Samaria?' (Jews do not share things in common with Samaritans.) Jesus answered her, 'If you knew the gift of God, and who it is that is saying to you, "Give me a drink," you would have asked him, and he would have given you living water.' (John 4:3b–10)

We view this account using a psychodynamic lens. Freud's seminal psychodynamic theory was later developed in various directions by Jung, Adler, Horney, Erikson, and by Object Relations theorists such as Guntrip, Winnicott, and Klein. One shared feature within this tradition is to focus on the defences people erect to keep painful memories and feelings from impinging upon their consciousness. The psychodynamic perspective assumes that this repressed material is not neutral, but rather tends to erupt and wreak havoc through repeating patterns of unhealthy behaviour. Psychodynamic therapy seeks to gradually erode maladaptive barriers to self-insight, facilitating the client's maturity, freedom and personal responsibility. This passage shows Jesus as a master of the psalmists' exhortation: 'You desire truth in the inward being' (Psalm 51:6). He uses a form of laddering technique (D. Rowe, 1987) to enable 'descent' into the need and pain hidden beneath the presenting symptoms.

In this account, Jesus travels through Samaria, a land normally avoided by Jews due to long-standing political and religious conflict. Tired from the journey, he sat down at a well in the town of Sychar. A woman, whose Samaritan roots would render her an 'outsider' in Jewish eyes, came to draw water. The well itself was a potent religious symbol; in the Jewish mind water represented the Torah, the law that gives life. Furthermore, this water was drawn from the well dug by the Patriarch Jacob (Israel) himself, symbolising the true water and the true law. The scene, charged with dramatic inter-group tension, is set.

Jesus asks the woman to give him a drink, a highly unusual request since Jews did not interact with the mixed-blood, religiously idiosyncratic Samaritans. A good, pious Jew would normally refuse to use the same cup or utensil that an unclean Samaritan touched. The idea of a man speaking with a woman at all, especially concerning the religious matters that ensued, appalled the disciples who eventually witnessed this encounter.

His request is a surprising and generous act of inclusion, overturning social barriers. She replies: ' "How is it that you, a Jew, ask a drink of me, a woman of Samaria?" ' (v. 9)

Side-stepping the defensive social labels she reinstates, Jesus 'ladders' directly to her deeper need and makes another generous offer: ' "If you knew the gift of God, and who it is that is saying to you, 'Give me a drink,' you would have asked him, and he would have given you living water." ' (v. 10)

His ambiguous reply weaves deeper meanings into her daily effort to draw water. Anchored in a practicality that they share, he speaks to her in rich, symbolic language: he asks her for a drink, but says he would give her living water. Living water refers to running water, a rare and precious commodity in this dry land. This water is used for ritual cleansing and washing away of stain. No water, even from this sacred well of Sychar, could be more valuable, delicious or thirst quenching than living water. These multi-layered allusions were not lost on the woman. Against all social rules, he offers the opportunity to probe in to deeper and more uncomfortable longings.

Yet in so doing, Jesus does not force her to comply, nor does he not take the superior position. Through his earlier request he had placed himself in a vulnerable position: ' "Give me a drink" '. She can refuse.

Empowered by his unusual mutuality, she parries his approach with a reasonable yet convenient misunderstanding. She says, ' "Sir, you have no bucket, and the well is deep" '.

Continuing this deflection, she shifts focus towards external, concrete details, which also seem designed to maintain the upper hand: ' "Where do you get that living water? Are you greater than our ancestor Jacob?" ' (v. 11–12)

In his pursuit of her deeper truth, Jesus treats her deflection as 'defection' in Enlightened Tit for Tat terms. He does not comply with her deflection, but continues to home in on her pain and hope for relief: ' "Everyone who drinks of this water will be thirsty again, but those who drink of the water that I will give them will never be thirsty." ' (v. 13–14)

As he holds her gaze, he perhaps sees a person in hiding. He waits for her to make the next move. She answers, ' "Sir, give me this water, so that I may never be thirsty and have to keep coming here to draw water." ' (v. 15)

Is this a partial self-disclosure, or is there a note of sarcastic disbelief in the prospect of having her daily chores alleviated? Jesus ignores her readiness for substitute 'filler'. He seeks her deeper truth, knowing that it is not possible to encounter truth from a place of hiding. Jesus' next move is sudden confrontation. He told her, ' "Go, call your husband, and come back." ' (v. 16)

Bull's eye. This abrupt turn unmasks her. She bravely returns truth for truth. The woman answered, 'I have no husband.' (v. 17)

This is her first honest statement. He rewards her first fully cooperative move and responds, in Enlightened Tit for Tat parlance, with immediate forgiveness. This takes the form of an affirmation that leads on to his belief that she is capable of even greater honesty. Jesus says affirmatively, ' "You are right in saying 'I have no husband.' For you have had five husbands, and the one you have now is not your husband. What you have said is true!" ' (v. 18)

The clarity of Jesus' interpersonal style through this rapid sequence of generosity, robust boundaries, and forgiveness reveals to this woman that her game is up. She acknowledges the accuracy of his insight: ' "Sir, I see that you are a prophet." ' (v. 19) But she defects once more, and erects a second line of defense, drawing on readily available inter-group religious arguments. She counters: ' "Our ancestors worshipped on this mountain, but you say that the place we must worship is in Jerusalem." ' (v. 20)

Jesus recognises this defensive manoeuvre, and he responds in order to correct and enlarge her spiritual vision that has been entrenched in correct places and pious procedures. Her religious vision, built on rules that maintain clear in-group and out-group boundaries, keep her in shame and guilt of her transgressions. He draws her towards a higher level of abstraction, towards a faith anchored in spirit and truth that will reward her forays into truthfulness: ' "the hour is coming when you will worship the Father neither on this mountain nor in Jerusalem... But the hour is coming, and is now here, when the true worshippers will worship the Father in spirit and truth, for the Father seeks such as these to worship him. God is spirit, and those who worship him must worship in spirit and truth." ' (vv. 21, 23–34)

The woman meets this with her own religious congruence, wearily but conveniently putting off disclosure till the end of time: ' "I know that Messiah is coming... When he comes, he will proclaim all things to us." ' (v. 25) Then in a stunning act of self-giving, he says, ' "I am he, the one who is speaking to you." ' (v. 26)

To a Samaritan woman of questionable repute, Jesus entrusts the fullness of his identity, a revelation not yet granted to anyone else. It was a generous gift of self-disclosure that she was inching towards, but could not accomplish, yet in spite of her weakness Jesus makes himself known: ' "I am he, the one who is speaking to you." '

This is the therapeutic exchange that gives her the courage to face who she is: ' "Come and see a man who told me everything I have ever done!" ' She does not shy away from the implications: ' "He cannot be the Messiah, can he?" ' (v. 29)

Though the nature of this psychodynamic lens is highly interpretive, through it we see this woman restored, not in a vacuum, but in the context of a face-to-face relationship.

The rules of this relationship invite trust through generosity and forgiveness, and require honesty through robust boundaries and clarity. Her subsequent transformation authenticated her testimony to those who knew of her previous way of life. As a result, 'They left the city and were on their way to him.' (v. 30)

The Invalid by the Pool of Bethesda: John 5:2—16

Now in Jerusalem by the Sheep Gate there is a pool, called in Hebrew Beth-zatha, which has five porticoes. In these lay many invalids–blind, lame, and paralyzed. One man was there who had been ill for thirty-eight years. When Jesus saw him lying there and knew that he had been there a long time, he said to him, 'Do you want to be made well?' The sick man answered him, 'Sir, I have no one to put me into the pool when the water is stirred up; and while I am making my way, someone else steps down ahead of me.' Jesus said to him, 'Stand up, take your mat and walk.' At once the man was made well, and he took up his mat and began to walk. Now that day was a sabbath. So the Jews said to the man who had been cured, 'It is the sabbath; it is not lawful for you to carry your mat.' But he answered them, 'The man who made me well said to me, 'Take up your mat and walk.'' They asked him, 'Who is the man who said to you, 'Take it up and walk'?' Now the man who had been healed did not know who it was, for Jesus had disappeared in the crowd that was there. Later Jesus found him in the temple and said to him, 'See, you have been made well! Do not sin any more, so that nothing worse happens to you.' The man went away and told the Jews that it was Jesus who had made him well. Therefore the Jews started persecuting Jesus, because he was doing such things on the sabbath. (John 5:2–16)

Here we read John 5 through a different psychological lens: the cognitive perspective. Cognitive psychology focuses on how people think, and has become a dominant paradigm in psychology since the 1970's. A wide range of experimental techniques are used to access how people understand, pay attention to, and remember information, as well as problem-solve and make decisions. It implicitly models the brain as an information processor, akin to the ubiquitous computer of our era. However, it is recognised that all cognition is also influenced, biased, and enriched by emotion and social processes. Cognitive therapy has shown considerable success in overcoming depression, and is at least as successful as drug treatments; but unlike drug therapy, it empowers the client with cognitive skills that can prevent the return of depression.

One helpful angle on depression concerns 'learned helplessness' (Maier and Seligman, 1976). This was first detected in dogs during a Pavlovian-type experiment. One group of animals were given electric shocks, but allowed the opportunity to escape them by moving to the other half of the cage. A second group of dogs were also given electric shocks but were not allowed any means of escaping them. After a time, the second set of dogs appeared to be resigned to receiving the shocks and showed no attempt to avoid them, even when new cage arrangements allowed for a means of escape. Later studies made it clear that both animals and humans who experience uncontrollable negative events (such as earthquakes, war, or personal trauma such as child or sexual abuse) may come to expect that any attempts will fail to change how things are, and so they no longer respond. They believe that there just is no point in doing anything because nothing will ever get better.

This kind of negative, biased thinking can keep a person trapped in depression. Aaron Beck's cognitive theory of depression (A. T. Beck, 1976; see also A. T. Beck, 1993) is one of the most definitive and well known. According to Beck, a negative triad of three negative thoughts plays like a tape recorder in the background of the depressed person's mind, trapping the person in a world of failure and isolation. These often- unconscious thoughts impinge on the self, making salient the person's own worthlessness, negative interactions with the world, and the inexorable hopelessness of the future. Its parallels with learned helplessness are evident: I am worthless and powerless, other people are selfish and mean, and the future will only get worse. These negative ways of thinking can be reinforced by further errors of logic that exaggerate the negative and discount the positive. For example:

- Arbitrary inference: drawing negative inferences with no supporting evidence (e.g., 'He didn't say hello to me, therefore he must be angry at me').
- Overgeneralization: making global assumptions about self-worth from a single fact (e.g., 'I didn't get an A on that exam, therefore I am a total failure').
- Magnifying or minimization: misconstruing the importance of events (e.g., 'I got an A this time, but only because it was an easy quiz').

We return to John 5. A man who had been an invalid for 38 years was lying there. The cause of his incapacitation is unclear; the Greek word does not necessarily mean a paralysis of the limbs. Jesus 'saw' this man and more; this motif of seeing is often used to denote a seeing into the whole person, and this attuning to the man's deeper condition is the overture for Jesus' generous move: ' "Do you want to be made well?" ' (v. 6)

By asking 'do you want?' Jesus pinpoints the vital aspect of this man's problem: his *inability* to use his will. The man answers, ' "Sir, I have no one to put me into the pool when the water is stirred up." ' (v. 7)

It appears that life has given this man ample material to construct a cage of learned helplessness for this man. The grievous losses of health and relationships over 38 long years resulted in isolation and hopelessness. The only source of hope in his worldview (the divine 'stirring' of the healing waters) is beyond reach, and these negative thought patterns have repeated at every failed attempt, meanwhile enforcing this man's belief in the ill will of others: ' "I have no one to put me into the pool when the water is stirred up; and while I am making my way, someone else steps down ahead of me." ' (v. 7)

From the man's reply, we can imagine an internal tape of Beck's negative triad playing in this man's mind: 'I am alone, others are uncaring and selfishly get the goods at my expense, and I will never get a chance in this unfair world'. Such thought patterns imprison a person in continuing depression and helplessness. The man's reply is a naked expression of need. It may also convey the man's unwillingness to risk again, or to ask for healing. If interpreted as such, this 'defection' is met with a sudden command: ' "Stand up, take your mat and walk." ' (v. 8)

The man's instant cooperation with this outlandish command merges with Jesus' generous power that reinstates him to life. At once the man was cured, and with this healing, the potential for demolishing this long-standing depressive mental cage also has unfurled.

Because this healing happened on the Sabbath, the Jewish authorities confront the man who had been healed: ' "It is the sabbath; it is not lawful for you to carry your mat." But he answered them, "The man who made me well said to me, 'Take up your mat and walk.'" ' (v. 10–11). Here we see the man still as a passive recipient of healing. It seems as if the man has not yet engaged with his own will, either in the building of his mental prison, nor of its dismantling. He seems to be saying, 'None of this is my doing.' And indeed, 'the man who had been healed did not know who it was, for Jesus had disappeared in the crowd.' (v. 13)

Later, Jesus seeks out this man again, finds him at the temple, and through this generous move, places himself at increased risk of being identified. The action is generous, but his statement is quite biting: ' "See, you have been made well! Do not sin any more, so that nothing worse happens to you." '

This is a curious, confrontational statement. Elsewhere in the gospels Jesus makes it very clear that there is no direct one-to-one relationship between personal sin and suffering, contrary to the pervading worldview of his time. Yet here, he seems to suggest that there is. We may speculate an indirect relationship is warranted: this man's self-destructive mental prison comprised sins against himself, and in a chain reaction, involved the sin of alienating others through his expectations of a hostile world.

Having thus sought out the man, and in an effort to enlighten him, warns him to repent (*metanoia*, to change one's mind). Jesus is now identified; this man can report him to the authorities. And the man does so!

It seems a curious act of ingratitude, but perhaps not surprising for one who still is placing responsibility in places and persons outside himself. We are uncertain whether the man ultimately received the all-encompassing generosity of the healing as ammunition to explode his imprisoning mental world. This would have required exercise of the will and the taking of responsibility for his thought patterns, however subliminal. This is something only the man himself could accomplish, not through mere optimism, but fuelled by the reality of his healing.

The Man with the Withered Hand: Luke 6:6—11

Lastly, we will look at a passage in Luke chapter 6 through the lens of the behaviourist perspective. In line with strict empiricism, the behaviourist approach confines itself to examining only observable, quantifiable behaviour. An early example of the approach is seen in Pavlov's work in the early twentieth century. He discovered how a neutral object (such as a door handle) can lose its neutrality after repeated pairings with an emotional state (such as fear). For example, a mother who is afraid of germs may slap a child's hand every time he touches a doorknob. Over time, simply seeing a doorknob can be enough to produce fear in the child.

Behaviourism's stance is that just as this pairing has been learned, so it can be unlearned, and on this basis are therapies constructed. During systematic desensitization (Wolpe, 1969), a trusted therapist accompanies the client to face the feared object in graduated doses (for example, the arachnophobic will first view photos of spiders, then spiders in a glass cage, and finally even touch a spider). In demonstrating calm in the face of the feared object, the therapist helps the client to find his or her own courage. A second, more risky technique is called flooding, where the client is given intense doses of the feared object or situation (Stampfl and Lewis, 1967). This too happens with the trusted therapist close at hand. When it is successful, clients find that they have survived the onslaught of the feared object, and that the fear itself has been diminished. Other behavioural problems, such as social isolation, can be helped by discovering what rewards are needed to reinforce the learning of appropriate social skills (Ullmann and Krasner, 1965). In this account in Luke 6, we see Jesus using tactics not too dissimilar whilst maintaining his interpersonal style again featuring generosity, robustness, forgiveness and clarity.

> On another sabbath he entered the synagogue and taught, and there was a man there whose right hand was withered. The scribes and the Pharisees watched him to see whether he would cure on the sabbath, so that they might find an accusation against him. Even though he knew what they were thinking, he said to the man who had the withered hand, 'Come and stand here.' He got up and stood there. Then Jesus said to them, 'I ask you, is it lawful to do good or to do harm on the sabbath, to save life or to destroy it?' After looking around at all of them, he said to him, 'Stretch out your hand.' He did so, and his hand was restored. But they were filled with fury and discussed with one another what they might do to Jesus. (Luke 6: 6–11)

The tension is set: it is another Sabbath, the day of rest. The reader is directed to the man's withered right hand, the hand normally used for work ('sinister' left hands in many cultures are left for unmentionable tasks). Work makes a person useful and confers a place in society, and physical imperfection was as a judgement from God or as a reason for exclusion from God's presence (for instance, priests who entered into God's holy presence were required to be free of physical imperfection). As such, this man would have endured economic, social, and to some degree, religious exclusion which could readily translate into feelings of inferiority as the individual internalises the avoidant or hostile reactions of others. We can imagine that this man may have learned to avoid drawing attention to himself, particularly to his withered hand. His avoidant behaviour over time may have fostered some dread of social exposure.

In this encounter, Jesus 'works a triangle' and engages with the Pharisees and the man. Aware that the Pharisees were watching closely to see if he would heal on the Sabbath, Jesus simultaneously confronts their legalism and the man's likely dread of exposure. 'Even though he knew what they were thinking', Jesus says to the man with the withered hand, ' "Come and stand here." ' (v. 8)

Is this, for the man, a terrifying experience akin to flooding? Yet something gives this man the courage to respond to Jesus' terrible request. Perhaps he has heard rumours of Jesus' healing power. The man comes forward in a gesture of ultimate cooperation. All eyes are fixed upon him; some glinting with the legal power to excommunicate him for involvement in 'work' on the Sabbath.

Jesus returns the Pharisees' hostile stare with a confrontation: ' "is it lawful to do good or to do harm on the sabbath, to save life or to destroy it?" ' (v. 9)

Met with silence, Jesus then responds to the man's trust and stretches that trust even further, saying: ' "Stretch out your hand." ' (v. 10)

Here is the ultimate risk: Jesus asks to see the man's imperfection, his shame, and his inferiority. The man took the risk, and his hand was restored. The man faced social exposure, and in the presence of Jesus, survived it to find that he was not only restored physically, but emotionally and socially as well.

Today, question marks rightly hover over flooding as a technique: what about its emotional cost? Jesus also had imposed 'flooding' on the Pharisees, those well-intentioned but oppressive experts of religion. He forced them to confront a redefinition of their role in protecting the Sabbath. As a result, 'they were filled with fury' (v. 11). In unmasking the man's debility and social exclusion, Jesus unmasked the harmful potential of religion to be rigid and self-serving. Jesus also unmasks himself; he is henceforth seen by the religious experts in a new, adversarial light.

Conclusion

Through these healing encounters, Jesus meets physical, emotional, cognitive, social and behavioural needs with accuracy and power. A strong current running throughout these accounts is the restoration of the individual to the community – often involving some change on the part of the community in order to embrace the poor, the socially outcast, or the previously excluded person. The therapeutic relationship demonstrated in these healing encounters provides a prototype for healthy social relationships, relationships made possible through the healing and reacceptance of the outcast. What can be said about the miraculous nature of the healings themselves? Although beyond comprehension, neither are these healings simply anti-rational, magical tricks. They are imbued with moral logic and power. Both the individual and something beyond the individual are made whole.

Two further elements are evident in these therapeutic encounters. The first is Jesus' sensitive attuning to each individual, which may account for the apparent lack of consistency in the content of his psychological approach. Through our application of three different 'best-fit' psychological lenses, Jesus apparently did not espouse a 'one size fits all' theoretic approach that we can tie down in modern psychological terms. He responds flexibly and creatively to each person and social context. And yet, the parallels between these healing accounts and the broad therapeutic goals of modern psychology are intriguing. What common ground underlies these different ways of conceptualising human experience?

From the first wrestling of psychology's foundational theorists, the discipline of modern psychology has developed largely from within Judeo–Christian culture with heavy influences from the Enlightenment. Given the evident common ground, it is reasonable to ask whether psychology as we know it might have developed the same way if it was positioned in a different religious or cultural context. While it is important to avoid conflating psychological and religious perspectives, it seems there are some deeply shared roots and fruits despite their trunks running along different sources of authority and according to distinct ways of knowing.

'Enlightened' Tit for Tat as a lens through which to view Jesus' interpersonal style not only reveals his robust boundaries, generosity, and forgiveness, it also focuses our attention to the genuine freedom he afforded to others to cooperate or defect. Jesus makes no attempt to manipulate, persuade, coerce or plead. He honours individual freedom, a feature vital to healthy relationships. This freedom is taken: some cooperate, others do not. Jesus accepts the consequences of their choices.

Second, it is clear that not all Jesus' interactions across the four gospels fit the Enlightened Tit for Tat model. Among notable exceptions are his interactions during his arrest, trial, torture and crucifixion. In these harrowing contexts, he often maintains silence and forbearance, seeming to cooperate in light of others' defection. The model also does not sit easily with his teaching that his disciples must deny themselves, pick up their cross and follow him.

In-group and out-group distinctions clarify to some degree why Enlightened Tit for Tat fits these healing encounters, but not all other gospel accounts. Towards members of his covenant in-group (Israel), Jesus may have expected the features of generosity, robustness, forgiveness and clarity to be part of healthy covenant life. According to this understanding, the scribes and Pharisees, towards whom Jesus was so famously insulting, are treated as members of his in-group (as is written in Proverbs 27:6, 'Well meant are the wounds a friend inflicts')! But towards outsiders, particularly towards Roman oppressors, Jesus chose an interpersonal strategy that shares a similar spirit but is distinct in outward appearance. To violence he responds with non-violence, not in abject submission, but to mirror back the wrong. He breaks the retributive cycle of violence and affords a moment of stillness in which evil can be seen for what it is. Is that perception accepted? Each individual involved has to decide.

Across the range of Jesus' interactions, we see him on the warpath against all that degrades human dignity and spiritual value. With flexibility and insight he takes the initiative against the social structures, deceptions, defenses, learned helplessness, negative thought patterns and paralysing fears that imprison us. He models an interpersonal style through which he insists on knowing the other, and on being known.

Author's note

The author wishes to thank Bonnie Zahl for her editing prowess, and Eolene Boyd-MacMillan and Mark Savage for comments on Enlightened Tit for Tat.

5

Fraser Watts

PERSONAL TRANSFORMATION

In this chapter, I will look at the gospels as a guide to personal transformation. I need to begin by clarifying my background assumption, that personal transformation is a point of common interest and concern between Christianity and contemporary culture. Admittedly, the language in which it is described, and the assumptions about how personal transformation comes about, may be different. However there seems no denying that both the Christian tradition and contemporary culture are much concerned with radical personal change (see also Watts, in press).

The New Testament talks about leaving behind an old life and embracing a new one. The new life is partly one of changed belief, partly one of spiritual union with Christ, partly a matter of becoming part of his body on earth, and partly a matter of moral transformation. For example, St Paul writes in his letter to the Ephesians: 'you were taught to put away your former way of life, your old self, corrupt and deluded by its lusts, and to be renewed in the spirit of your minds, and to clothe yourselves with the new self, created according to the likeness of God in true righteousness and holiness' (Eph. 4:22–3). There is no doubt that St Paul's language about the old and the new is speaking of personal transformation.

Personal transformation is also a central theme in much of contemporary culture, particularly prominent in America, but increasingly important elsewhere. Part of the pervasive influence of psychotherapy on our culture is that it has engendered a concern with personal growth, with how people can develop so as to handle their problems and limitations better. Increasingly, people are not content with themselves as they are, but are in search of ways to become better, more fulfilled people.

It is understandable why people should seek personal transformation. For many, life seems a wearisome grind, with many demands that bring no real fulfilment. They become fed up with relationships that go wrong, or with the loneliness that is an alternative to relationships. They long for a way of living that will give them a spring in their steps, and a way of relating to people that is life-giving and liberating.

People have no doubt always wanted these things. However, as basic material needs have now been met, at least to a minimally satisfactory degree for the vast majority of people in the West, individuals are looking beyond these basic needs to higher personal needs. Maslow (1964) has theorised about this in terms of a hierarchy of needs: as lower-level basic needs are met, people increasingly seek higher-level needs of personal transformation and fulfilment.

Of course, some have argued that there is a radical difference between how Christianity and the contemporary personal growth movement approach these matters (Vitz, 1977). The former's view of fulfilment is God-centred, whereas the latter's view is human-centred. The personal growth movement looks at humanity with a rosy glow, whereas Christianity understands the need for repentance in order that transformation can occur. Clearly, there are differences between the two, but this kind of sharp contrast can end up caricaturing both. Even where there appear to be differences, it its debatable how deep they go. They may be relatively superficial differences in the language that people use to describe things, or more they may be fundamental differences about the process of transformation. My advice is to take a balanced view of this issue, and to be alert to both similarities and differences between how Christianity has traditionally approached personal transformation, and how it is approached in contemporary culture. There is, however, no doubt that personal transformation is a central theme in both.

Then and Now

In this chapter, I will focus on the gospels, and the story and teaching of Jesus that they embody, as a guide to personal transformation. That immediately raises the question of whether the gospels were intended to be read in this way, or whether this is an anachronistic misreading of them, imposing the mindset of Western culture at the beginning of the third millennium onto texts that emerged from Palestine 2000 years ago.

Again, I would like to take a balanced approach to that issue. On the one hand, it is true that the gospels are certainly not dealing with personal transformation in the sense that the contemporary West understands it. We tend to detach the individual from wider society and focus solely on the individual, whereas they saw transformation as affecting everything; it was a radical and universal transformation that affected both individual and society. Also, the evangelists who wrote the gospels did not see themselves as writing texts about personal transformation, and would have been surprised by the suggestion that they were. On the other hand, I would claim that issues are raised in the gospels that transcend the culture from which they came. Perhaps the evangelists didn't think they were writing about personal transformation, but it may still part of the purposes of God that the gospels should provide a guide to personal transformation.

To avoid misunderstanding, I am not claiming that there is timeless teaching about personal transformation in the gospels that transcends cultural origins and is able to speak to any culture. The gospels come from one culture; we live in another. However, recognising that difference, it is still fair to ask what the gospels have to say about what we would now call 'personal transformation'. My claim is that, speaking across the divide of time and space, the gospels have something interesting, important and radical to say about this contemporary preoccupation.

The theme of transformation comes up in many ways in the gospels and is apparent in at least four ways: Jesus' actions, his relationships, his teaching and in his own experience of personal change.

Jesus' Promise of Transformation

Many of the actions of Jesus provide a metaphor for personal transformation. That is true of the seven big stories in St John's gospel (chapters 2—11) often known as the 'signs of glory'. For example, Jesus takes water and transforms it into wine. That can be heard as a parable of how ordinary people (who are like water) can be taken by Jesus and transformed into something analogous to the best wine that the guests at the wedding have ever drunk. It is a telling point in the story that Jesus does not just produce excellent wine from nowhere. He takes what is available, the ordinary water that they have to hand, and orders that the jars be filled to the brim with it before he undertakes his work of transformation.

Similarly, in the story of the feeding of thousands of people with a few loaves, Jesus takes what is available, the handful of loaves that have been brought into the desert, and transforms them into superabundance, plenty for everyone and much left over. Heard as a parable about personal transformation, it seems that Jesus is saying that if we feel we have depleted resources and not enough time and energy to cope, he has the ability to take what time and energy we have and to transform it into plenty.

The gospel stories about personal encounters with Jesus deal more explicitly with personal transformation. Numerous people

in the gospels meet Jesus and are transformed by their encounter
with him.

One intriguing story is that of Nathanael (John 1:43–51).
Nathanael, who is brought to Jesus by Philip, is initially sceptical. He has assumptions about different kinds of people, what
we would now call stereotyping. As far as he is concerned,
Nazareth is a small and unimportant town, and no significant
person is likely to come from it. However, his encounter with
this particular Nazarene undermines his prejudices, as
assumptions about people of different age, race, nationality,
gender or sexual orientation are often undermined by a real and
personal encounter, in which we find our stereotypes
disconfirmed.

Nathanael's relationship with Jesus is built on the Nathanael's
feeling that he is intimately known and understood by Jesus.
Jesus pays him the compliment of calling him 'an Israelite in
whom there is no deceit' (v. 47). It is not quite clear whether
Jesus is being serious or tongue in cheek, but Nathanael takes it
seriously; he is astonished that Jesus, whom he has never previously met, has arrived at such an astute perception of what
kind of person he is! It is a story that speaks movingly of Jesus as
an acute observer of persons, and of the deep importance to all of
us of feeling known and understood.

Then Jesus utters words of deep promise. Jesus' particular
insight into Nathanael's character is only the beginning; if
Nathanael follows Jesus there will be much more than intimate
insight. Indeed, harking back to the Old Testament for a powerful image, he tells Nathanael that he will see 'heaven opened up
and the angels of God ascending and descending upon the Son
of Man' (v. 51). These are words that speak to our deepest
dreams and longings. Jesus is promising us that our fondest
hopes, the ones that we might have assumed could never be
realised, can actually come true if we follow him. These words
undermine the cynical and disillusioned mind-set often passed
for being 'realistic'.

The story cuts off at that point, and we are never told what the impact was on Nathanael as he followed Jesus, and if so whether his dreams came true. At least, if we believe Jesus' assessment of him, he was a person of integrity, and that is a strong foundation on which to build a deeper personal transformation.

Many of Jesus' encounters are characterised by such radical words of insight and promise. For example, to Nicodemus (John 3), an educated man who comes to Jesus with deep curiosity, Jesus talks about how he can be 'born again', a phrase that has entered the linguistic currency of evangelical Christianity. There is an interesting parallel with the process of 're-birthing' that has come out of gestalt therapy. There are many differences between the two, but it is interesting to find contemporary counselling talking in its own way about being 'born again'.

Similarly, to the woman Jesus meets at the well (John 4) he talks about how he is living water. He promises that if she drinks of such water she will never be thirsty again because streams of water will well up within her. It is a theme to which Jesus returns, extending these words of promise to everyone when he speaks in Jerusalem on the last day of the festival (John 7:37–8): ' "Let anyone who is thirsty come to me, and let the one who believes in me drink. As the Scripture has said, "out of the believer's heart shall flow rivers of living water." "' For those who feel that they have inadequate resources to cope with the demands of life and are feeling depleted, these are almost extravagant words of hope and encouragement.

Though this theme of promise is particularly featured in John's gospel, it is by no means confined to them. For example, he speaks words of promise to the four fishermen who become his first disciples. This is particularly clear in Luke's gospel where that calling is linked to the story of Jesus telling them to let down their nets on the other side after they have been fishing all night and caught nothing. Upon following Jesus' instructions, the fishermen's catch was so great that their nets were about to break (Luke 5:1–11). The message of promise is again clear. Without Jesus, the experience of life is one of depletion and lack of fulfilment; with Jesus there is a promise of super-abundance.

Making the Psychology of the Gospels Explicit

Let us now turn to recasting this message in psychological thinking. The clearest analogy is found in Jungian psychology. Indeed, many of Jung's central ideas can be seen as a secularised recasting of the religious message, though Jesus would probably not have comfortably accepted it. Jung makes a distinction between the ego and what he calls Self. The word 'Self' needs to be approached with caution here, because Jung uses it in a way that is very different from how it is normally used; it is often spelt with a capital S to mark the fact that it is a technical term.

It is the contrast between ego and Self that is important in Jung's thought. He takes over from Freud the concept of the ego, which is the centre of our conscious life. Self, in contrast, embraces our unconscious life as well. That is partly a matter of the personal unconscious, the aspects of our own personality that we choose not to notice because they are difficult or painful, what Jung calls the 'shadow' side of our personality. However, it also includes the collective unconscious that we share with others, a world that is peopled with kinds of figures that crop up repeatedly in the human psyche, such as the Great Mother or the Eternal Youth. As far as the contrast between ego and Self is concerned, the key point is that the ego is limited to our conscious life, whereas Self embraces the totality of our psychic lives, conscious and unconscious. Ego is limited, but Self represents wholeness.

Self is therefore in one sense a goal towards which we move in our personal journey, a journey that Jung calls 'individuation'. However, the Self is more than just the end point to which the journey is moving. It also has the power to help us on the journey; it has a way of announcing itself to the ego, drawing our attention to what we can become and inspiring us to move on the journey towards it. The Self 'calls' the ego towards it, rather as Jesus calls his disciples to him.

Jung's contrast between ego and Self resonates with much Christian teaching: a calling to the individual towards transformation. His ideas seem to have been derived in large measure from the Christian thinking that is deeply embedded in our culture, even if it is not always explicitly acknowledged. In many ways, Jung's ideas are Christian thinking recast in apparently secular form, but in a way that falls fresh on the ears and can jolt us into seeing more clearly what was in Christian thinking all along (see Bryant, 1983; Edinger, 1972).

How secular is it? Some will say that Jung's psychology is about nothing more than our own internal psychological journey and has nothing to do with God. That is, however, a mistaken view; Jung is explicit about the link between Self and God. Self is an image of God in the psyche, and speaks to us of God. That is reminiscent of what Christians say about humans being created in the image of God, and our being given his Spirit as a gift to live within us; the Holy Spirit really is God, but nevertheless lives within us to the extent that he becomes part of us. Just as the Self speaks to us of God, the Holy Spirit reveals to us the things that 'no eye has seen, no ear has heard, no mind has conceived what God has prepared for those who love him' (1 Cor. 2:9).

One difference is that Christians are emphatic about the reality of God beyond the psyche, whereas Jung tends to say that all he can do as a psychologist is to describe what he finds in the psyche. Certainly, he finds an image of God there, but whether there is a God beyond that he regards as something that as something not proper for him as a mere psychologist to comment on. It is also worth noting that Jung is emphatic about the limitations of the ego. For him, if we live an ego-bound life there is no possibility of wholeness or fulfilment. He could not be stronger about the importance of people leaving behind their ego-bound life. This echoes Jesus calling people to leave behind their old lives, as fishermen, tax-gatherers or whatever, and follow him.

The analogy can be developed a little further. When Jesus tells Nathanael he will see heaven opened if he followed Jesus, it is like the Self saying to the ego that it will find unbelievable richness if it has the courage to give up its limited existence and embark on the journey to wholeness and fulfilment. Jung's contrast between ego and Self is parallel to the contrast in the gospels between earth and heaven. Jesus' encouragement to Nicodemus to leave his earth-bound life behind and see the possibilities of heaven (John 3) is like Jung encouraging us to leave our ego-bound life behind and see the possibilities of Self. In both cases, this seems to depend on establishing a connection between the two. Jesus talks about angels ascending and descending between earth and heaven, thus providing a regular linkage between them. In a parallel way, Jung talks about having a healthy axis between and ego and Self in which the ego recognises its limitations but has enough healthy connection with the Self to be able to move towards it.

To the fishermen whom Jesus called to follow him, it probably seemed futile to let down their nets again after they had caught nothing all night. It might also seem risky to the fishermen to let their nets down deep into the sea after having just failed. Similarly, to the ego it can seem pointless to aspire to life beyond itself. It can also seem risky to let go of secure foundations and embark on the journey towards Self, the image of God in the psyche. However, if we can overcome the sense that it is either futile or too risky, the potential rewards are a very great. Jesus spoke to the woman at the well about how it would be like water always welling up within her. Similarly, once the ego finds the connection with Self, it finds it is drawing on resources of undreamt of richness. It is like rebirthing, or being born again as Jesus put it to Nicodemus.

It might be objected that in talking about the promise Jesus holds out to people in terms of personal transformation, I have presented Jesus' mission in overly individualistic terms. I would accept that the transformation Jesus promises is a much broader one, including a transformation of society as well. However, I believe that Jesus' promise is in part one for the individual. Talking about it in terms of personal transformation is not the whole picture, but I believe it is definitely part of the promise Jesus holds out toward us.

The Challenge of Transformation

Jesus begins his encounters with people by opening up possibilities, but he also repeatedly emphasises that there is a personal cost in accepting his invitation and following his path. That cost is apparent in his encounters with particular individuals, such as the rich young man who wanted to know what he would have to do to enter the kingdom of heaven, and was told he would have to go and sell all his possessions. However the costliness is laid out most clearly in Jesus' general teaching.

At the heart of Jesus' teaching is the concept of 'metanoia', a fundamental reordering of attitudes and mind-set. It is often translated into English as 'repentence', though that makes it sound too negative and doom-laden. Nevertheless, Jesus never disguises the fact that, if we want to embrace new attitudes and values, old ones need to be abandoned. As he says, you can't put new wine into old skins. He warns people that if they are to embrace his new world order, his 'kingdom', that has to be their overriding priority. He says it is like searching for a really fine pearl and having to sell everything else in order to purchase it.

A particularly interesting saying of Jesus', from this point of view, is 'those who would find their life will lose it, and those who lose their life for my sake will find it' (Matt. 10:39). It is interesting, first of all, to note that the Greek word that is translated as 'life' is 'psyche', and while it certainly does mean physical life it also has overtones of mind-set. This saying is best read as referring to both. As always, Jesus wants people to find their life/psyche. However, he warns us that, paradoxically, we will need to lose our life/psyche in order to re-find it.

That raises the question of what kind of life is to be laid down and what is to be taken up. Using the concepts of ego and Self that we have just been considering, it seems that it is the life of the ego that has to be laid down if the more complete life of the Self is ever to be found. Many of the Beatitudes can be heard as saying something similar, particularly the first one, 'Blessed are the poor in spirit'. Starting from our limited ego-bound form of existence, we need to acknowledge its poverty before we can move on to anything higher.

In personal transformation, as with following Jesus, it is necessary to leave behind old ways of thinking and behaving. There are often understandably mixed feelings about this. When people are locked in a maladaptive mode of existence, they usually genuinely want to move on to something more fulfilling, but are also in some ways reluctant to leave behind old patterns to which they have grown accustomed.

For example, people who are depressed usually have a very negative view of themselves, the world around them, and the future. It is crucial to overcoming depression to leave behind those negative patterns of thought. However, it can seem risky to do that; a more positive outlook seems to carry the risk of disappointment. Equally, when people become locked in maladaptive patterns of relationship, things can become very twisted. After many years of being treated badly, it is hard to believe that anyone who treated us better would be genuine in what they were doing. There can be something comforting about receiving the sympathy and concern of others, and even in feeling sorry for oneself. Personal transformation often requires letting go of these ways of living.

In calling people to a radically new way of thinking and being, Jesus understands that they need to 'repent' of their present ways if they are to really leave them behind. Personal transformation in its own way requires a similar kind of repentance. The bad old ways can become compulsive, and Jesus understands the radical renunciation of the past that is called for if people are to break free and reach for the higher ground that he promises them.

Resources for Transformation

That challenging message is accompanied, in the teaching of Jesus, by a message of encouragement. It is central to Jesus' message that people are not called to make a break for a new and better life on their own, or out of their own resources. Jesus talks encouragingly about his new way of being, his 'kingdom', having already been inaugurated; he asks people to read the signs and see the evidence. He refers back to the signs the prophets had said would accompany the 'time of deliverance' to which they had looked forward, and Jesus points out that all these things are already happening around him.

The message is not 'let's get together and start a kingdom'; it is 'the kingdom has already begun, come and join in'. Psychologically, there is a huge difference between the two. It is a message nicely captured in Sydney Carter's well known hymn, 'Lord of the dance', especially in the chorus, 'Dance then wherever you may be; I am the Lord of the dance said he, and I'll lead you all, wherever you may be, and I'll lead you all in the dance, said he' (Carter, 1963). Jesus invites people to join in his dance that has already begun; he doesn't just tell them to take to the floor on their own.

This message is also clear in those well-known words of Jesus, 'this is my commandment, that you love one another as I have loved you' (John 13:34). Loving other people is not easy for any of us, and our ability to do it seems to depend critically on the amount of love that we have received ourselves. Those who have known little affection themselves find it very hard to show it to other people. Psychologically, it is very significant that Jesus doesn't simply tell people to find the resources for love within themselves; he first surrounds them with his own love and tells them to show similar love to other people.

In a parallel way, as the Lord's Prayer makes clear, a forgiveness of other people is intertwined with God's forgiveness of us. This is something that is sometimes neglected in the current enthusiasm for forgiveness therapy, very helpful though that is in many ways. People who would benefit from forgiving others do not always have the personal resources to undertake it, and sometimes need to experience forgiveness themselves before they can forgive others.

The way in which Jesus promises that his Spirit will remain with his followers after his crucifixion underlines this message in yet another way. Jesus had not started something that his followers will then have to carry on by themselves. Even after his earthly death the gift of his living Spirit will provide them with the resources to carry on. So, the message comes back full circle to the positive way in which it began, with the promise that 'out of the believer's heart shall flow rivers of living water' (John 7:37). St John's gospel goes on to explain that when he said that, Jesus was talking about the gift of his Spirit.

In a similar way, personal transformation does not normally happen with people working at things on their own. Useful progress can be made, for example, through people reading self-help books, but the deepest personal transformation requires the context of a relationship. That is often the most important role of a counsellor, not to offer insights or guidance, but to provide the relational context in which people can undertake personal transformation. As Carl Rogers put it, every good counsellor needs to convey a positive regard for the person they are working with, empathic understanding of them, and to do that in a way that is manifestly genuine and sincere (Rogers, 1951). What people need in counselling is someone who can relate to them like that, more than they need practical wisdom about their problems.

It is also significant that people's capacity for showing courage is massively enhanced if they do things with others. In trench warfare, for a lonely soldier to go 'over the top' by himself is much more difficult than a wave of people doing it together. Warfare depends on this group psychology, but there is a similar but more benign group psychology of being involved in Jesus' kingdom. The Church, at its best, is a community of people who are together finding the courage to love one another as they have been loved.

A major part of 'faith' is recognising and accepting that we don't have to do things on our own, but are being offered the resources that make it possible. It is of little help for those resources to be available unless we recognise them and have confidence in them, and that is precisely what faith is. Similarly, in counselling, it helps enormously if people begin believing that their therapist will enable them to change, and hoping and expecting that transformation will happen. The terminology is different, but some kind of 'faith' is equally important both in following Jesus and in personal transformation.

Jesus as a Model of Transformation

There is yet another way in which the gospels provide a guide to personal transformation, which is that Jesus serves as a model of someone who is himself undergoing that transformation. He provides an example, which encourages people to believe in the possibility, and implicitly provides guidance on how to go about it. Jesus himself seems to have undergone the kind of journey of personal change that Jung called individuation. Jesus is a model of an 'individuating ego'.

The value of Jesus as a model for our personal journeys is often blunted by assuming that Jesus required no transformation. However, Jesus was not born with a fully conscious sense of being the unique son of his heavenly Father; the snapshot in Luke's gospel of Jesus at twelve reveals him with a developing sense of his special relationship to his heavenly Father. Equally, through his public ministry, Jesus has a growing sense of the sacrifice that he will have to make at the end of it, and he braces himself to do what has to be done.

We have seen how Jesus' encounters with people usually begin with his holding out the promise of unexpected possibilities opening up for them and of their deepest longings being fulfilled. His invitation reflects his knowledge and appreciation of them as they are, and as what they could be. In a parallel way, Jesus' own public ministry begins with a powerful sense of endorsement of who he is, and of the possibilities before him. This happened as Jesus was baptised. It seems that as he was lifted up by John the Baptist out of the waters of the River Jordan he had one of those powerful 'religious experiences' that change everything; he understood in a new and vivid way his relationship to his heavenly Father, and the course of action that would flow from that. Of course, there were difficult moments ahead. However it seems that at that moment Jesus himself experience something like what he promised Nathanael; he saw the ' "heaven opened and the angels of God ascending and descending upon the Son of Man." '

We have seen next how Jesus tells people bluntly that those who follow him will need to leave their old lives behind. It begins with renunciation, as it does for Jesus himself. His personal experience of this comes in the desert to which he goes immediately after his baptism. What he experiences there is the fine difference between right and wrong ways of fulfilling his mission. It is a kind of completion of the learning of the 'knowledge of good and evil' at which Adam and Eve snatch prematurely in the story told in Genesis chapter three.

Jesus learns in the desert not to turn stones into bread. However, in his subsequent ministry, he is able to take a handful of loaves and use them to feed several thousand people. Similarly, from a mountain top in the wilderness Jesus is offered all the lands he can see as part of his kingdom, but on returning from the desert be establishes his 'kingdom of heaven'. Finally, Jesus in the desert learns to resist the temptation to throw himself off the pinnacle of the temple, though at the culmination of his ministry he is able to return to a new form of life after his crucifixion, albeit with his hands and feet still scarred.

Finally, Jesus never feels he has to act alone, simply drawing on his own resources. Throughout his work he has such a powerful sense of unity with his heavenly Father that he feels they are inseparable. Just as all personal change seems to be facilitated by a transforming relationship, so what Jesus does is made possible by his sense of unity with his heavenly Father, and his complete confidence in him.

So, I hope I have shown the remarkable parallel between the issues of personal transformation raised in the gospels and in our contemporary culture. It is not that they are saying exactly parallel things at every point. However, there is a close enough similarity for there to be a fruitful dialogue about personal transformation between the two. Above all, I want to emphasise how Jesus is a powerful agent of transformation, both for those who encountered him in his life in Palestine, and for those who know him now through the gospels and personal experience. His threefold approach to transformation is to hold out a future better than we had dared to hope for, to warn us of the renunciation involved if it is to come true, and to reassure us that we will not be alone in following this path.

6

Beaumont Stevenson

TURNING TABOO ON ITS HEAD

Psychotherapy often involves seeing things in a fresh light. It is an exercise in turning problems round, so that things we thought were unacceptable or intolerable becomes not only acceptable, but can even become a source of blessing. The gospels also turn things round, and this chapter will draw some parallels between psychotherapy and Christianity in this regard. Specifically, it will focus on how the Bible systematically turns taboos on their head, and will explore some of the implications of that for personal change and renewal.

The work of a psychotherapist is not only to turn trauma into a memory, but also to assist in transformation. In many cases a personal tragedy becomes the basis of a greater understanding and compassion for others who suffer. Personal tragedy can be turned into help for others and lead to a deepening of compassion. The priest may give pastoral care and support in much the same way, but perhaps focusing more on what the individual wishes to make the centre of his or her life, and on the relationship of the events in the person's life to his or her faith.

The essential work of the priest is to comfort the afflicted and to afflict the comforted, to help people to turn their difficulties to their advantage. There are two working principles that we need to note about this:

1. Turning the unacceptable into the acceptable is the opposite of scapegoating. Scapegoating is when we make another person, or a particular group of people (or literally a goat in the Old Testament), responsible for our unacceptable feelings.
2. When we do something together as a group, it is so powerful that it can transform the unacceptable into a thing of beauty or desirability.

Seeing how Scripture turns taboos on their head will involve reading it in a new light. Our mind-set, or prejudice, determines what we can and cannot see in Scripture. If we looked at Scripture as a stranger might, with fresh eyes, what would we see which would surprise us? What are the particular dynamics running through God's relationship with us which characterise the overall pattern of the Gospel message? In order to see Scripture afresh, we may have to make the familiar strange. Often in reading Scripture we look for what we recognise and gloss over the rest. I am determined to look at Scripture and life afresh, and to see where the surprises are.

This was demonstrated for me in a social psychology class at university. We were exploring the nature of prejudice by being shown a picture of some passengers on a bus and were asked to study it carefully at our desks. We then were asked to turn the picture over and write what we had observed. The picture included a sweet looking granny and a vicious-looking thug sitting next to each other. Most of us observed the granny knitting and the thug carrying a gun. However, when we turned the picture over, we noticed, when it was pointed out to us, that it was the granny who had the 38-calibre pistol in her open handbag and the thug was knitting some baby apparel. Our prejudice therefore kept us from observing things correctly. This experience helped me take account of my preconceptions in reading Scripture, and I began to read in order to register the surprises in Scripture, rather than with the attitude 'Yes, I've read all this before, I know exactly what it says.' I have found that the surprises still register, no matter how familiar the portion of Scripture, and I have found God most often speaking in the surprises, rather than in the familiar.

Moving Beyond Respectability

As a psychotherapist and priest, I am aware of the general view that religion supports the status quo, and everything that religious people feel is 'nice' or socially desirable. This is a prejudice, and confuses religion with what psychologists call the superego. The superego is the culturally assimilated set of norms about what is right; it is the voice in the head that says, 'What would other people think?' Many people build their whole lives around assumptions about what other people think, and they assume that the church supports them in doing so. That conflates what is 'nice' with what is 'religious', and makes what is 'nice' a guide for the actions in their lives. Equally, it is assumed that anything that is not nice could not possibly be religious.

There is an essential difference between superego and moral conscience. Superego is based on admired or idealised models of behaviour as well as the rules and regulations of society and our own particular cultural group. If the superego is too rigid, the individual becomes inhibited and unhappy. If it is too lax it leads to immature and irresponsible behaviour. Moral conscience, in contrast is concerned with religious or ethical rights and wrongs. Both moral conscience and superego inflict pain in the form of guilt when transgressed.

The two frequently get confused and individuals feel that both carry equal moral weight because the guilt feels the same. The therapist attempts to lift the weight of unnecessary superego, and the priest can define what is appropriate or inappropriate to worry about. This distinction has not been emphasised enough in the teachings within theological colleges and the Church, and as a result, many Christians are left with a feeling of perpetual guilt rather than the joy of being free. Jesus too, attempted to lift guilt by breaking the Sabbath law and eating grain on the Sabbath, and explaining his actions in Matthew 12:1–8.

Compliance with what is 'nice' exercises a heavy tyranny because it leaves people feeling guilty for having the normal human feelings of anger, sensuality, or doubt. These are human experiences that Christians often avoid addressing. We all have to struggle with our human feelings or desires that may not always be 'nice', and Jesus must have struggled with them as well. Think of the pressures that his community must have put on him: 'Jesus, be a good boy; support your widowed mother by staying at home and running your father's carpentry shop; get married and have children and grandchildren; don't be rude to religious authorities; don't upset the status quo or the Roman occupying authority; it will only make it worse for the rest of us'. What would have happened if he had made these norms the guiding principles of his life? Though we are only speculating, such norms may have put a great deal of pressure on him given his identity as the Son of God and the Messiah.

When we read the gospels, our sense of 'niceness' and our emphasis on respectability can get in the way of seeing how God acts. For instance, had Jesus thrown the money-changers out of the temple in contemporary Britain, he might be taken to court and served with an ASBO (Anti Social Behaviour Order). How does this relate to the popular view of Jesus as being perfect, law-abiding and 'nice' to everyone? When we read this portion of Scripture, we may not register his behaviour, because we see him as a model (in superego terms) for our respectable behaviour.

What is the scriptural antidote against superego and respectability taking over? There is a basic Christian principle in the gospels, which is exemplified in the phrase: 'The stone that the builders rejected has become the cornerstone' (Matt. 21:42). This is also seen in Mary's Magnificat: 'He has brought down the powerful from their thrones, and lifted up the lowly' (Luke 1:52).

In the gospels, Jesus is critical of people who are proud and self satisfied, who think 'It's all sorted out; we have all the answers; God will not give us any surprises. We have got him down to a formula; just follow the rules!' Such thinking is spiritual death, because it rules out seeing a living God at work in unexpected ways, and we limit our perceptions of God at work to our own pre-determined formula, to our own idea of what is 'good'.

In Scripture, God has his own way of stopping things from getting in a rut. In the Old Testament, when Israel became proud, God led them into exile as an antidote or corrective spiritual experience. The Israelites wandered through the desert, with one day's food at a time, which made them more humble and more aware of God's daily providence. When they forgot God, they were sent into exile into Babylon, with the same result. The essence of Christianity is that in order to remain spiritual, we need to be wrong-footed, to see (and not ignore) the contradictions of life, and to get used to paradox.

In the Lord's Prayer we find the phrase, 'Give us this day our daily bread' (Matt. 6:11). In short, it is a prayer that leads us to take one day at a time and to depend on providence. In the Old Testament, this is called 'wandering'. If we continue wandering, we will be aware of God, whether that involves finding God during times of ill-health, doubt, or exile. The opposite of 'wandering' is to be 'landed'. Once we have stability, property and position, we become less aware of God and more interested in maintaining the status quo, planning our own lives and deciding for ourselves what is right and wrong. The essence of spirituality is to keep turning things on its head, to keep life from getting in a rut of self-righteous expectation.

Transforming and Reversing Taboo

If we were to identify a single basic, unifying working principle within Christianity, it would have to be transformation. The theme of transformation runs through most of the Christian dynamic: grit transformed into pearls, death into life, caterpillars into butterflies, taboos into sacraments. In Christianity, the essential transformation begins in the taboos, in the rejection of the shadow side of personality and of the unconscious in oneself and society. These are then changed into the spiritual core pillars around which Christianity is built: 'The stone that the builders rejected has become the cornerstone'.

Let us look at the main taboos which we hold as a society: cannibalism, incest, infanticide/ritual child abuse, death, psychopathology, and perhaps, as some Christians feel, homosexuality. We will see how these negative bits of grit are transformed into spiritual pearls through the loving action of God. The transformation of these into something spiritually beautiful and uplifting is precisely the pattern of the transforming work of spirituality, which uses the unacceptable and the tragic as opportunities for change.

Cannibalism

In primitive tribes the strength of one's enemies or of powerful leaders is absorbed by eating their flesh. Similarly, Christians take on strength by 'swallowing the leader'. Jesus invites us to 'eat his flesh and drink his blood' (see John 6:54–6). The Holy Communion as the central act of the Church is sacramental cannibalism, a transformation of something considered repugnant into the central spiritual act of the Church. A mother who adores her child often says, 'You are so beautiful I could just eat you all up' and playfully bites the child's tummy to its delighted giggles. We smile and nod in approval at this loving gesture, without consciously registering the implied cannibalistic content, but 'knowing what she means'. Love desires to take the other person inside ourselves and merge with them, making them part of us. It is one of the greatest taboos if taken too literally. Yet it forms the basis of one of the most spiritually nourishing acts of the Church.

Incest

God is our Father; he created us. He also created the Virgin Mary. The Church celebrates that Mary was impregnated by God (her Father) and so, technically in this incestuous act, Mary is both Jesus' mother and his sister. It is around this act that both the Annunciation (celebrated on 25 March, nine months before Christmas) and Christmas are celebrated. In this act, God's coming to earth is celebrated, without us registering the underlying taboo around which it is formed.

Adultery

Solomon, the greatest of all Jewish Kings, was the product of an adulterous relationship between David and Bathsheba.

Infanticide/Ritual child abuse

In the Old Testament, God asks Abraham to sacrifice his son Isaac. At the last moment, he stops Abraham from killing his son. We read the last minute saving of Isaac with relief. This contrasts with the Church, on Good Friday, celebrating the demonstration of God's love for us in allowing his own son to die on the cross. God rescues Isaac, but he does not rescue his own Son, allowing him to die so that a resurrection can take place. This is transformation of something abhorrent (child abuse) into a central spiritual demonstration of God's love for us.

Death

Death is normally feared as the end point at which our existence is terminated, or freeze-framed in time. However, in light of the resurrection, death is seen as an entrance into a new life. 'What you sow does not come to life unless it dies' (1 Cor. 15:36). We therefore call perhaps the worst day Jesus ever had to endure, not the 'worst Friday' but 'Good Friday', because after that day of transformation we no longer think of death as being the universally-feared last word.

Psychopathology

The adorable grandchild who melts your heart is baptised on the premise that inside is a basic core of self-centeredness, 'original sin', which is washed away by the baptism of the child. That gurgling baby also has the potential, as an adult, to have road-rage, strike one of her children in anger, and be self-centred. Lest we think otherwise, just watch the baby's face screw up in rage when it is hungry. However, the original and all-pervading sinfulness that is in the baby is ceremonially drowned in baptism, and rises again to new life, demonstrating that God can transform even the original sin within us.

Transforming Homosexuality into the Acceptable

A similar thing of turning taboo upside down happened with homoerotic behaviour being publicly sanctioned and labelled as 'good agricultural practice' during Old Testament times. How homoeroticism is seen in the Old Testament is a complex matter and is interpreted in different ways by different scholars. In what follows, I have chosen to explore the interpretation that I think makes most sense. Those who want to explore scholarly debates more fully should consult Nissinen (1998).

There is an often-quoted passage of Scripture from the book of Leviticus condemning homosexual practice: 'If a man lies with a male as with a woman, both of them have committed an abomination; they shall be put to death; their blood is upon them' (Lev. 20:13). This section of Scripture has a different style from the other part of Leviticus and is often called the 'H' source, or Holiness source. It may have been written between 600 and 570 BC, during the last days of the first temple and the first days of the Babylonian exile (i.e. at the end of a long period in which male cult prostitution was practiced). Until 600 BC there was no injunction against homosexual practice in Israel. It seems to have been added later, just before the Babylonian exile, and was probably intended specifically to end the male cult practice that had taken place in the temple in Jerusalem.

Male temple prostitution had been introduced when the Israelites entered the promised land of Canaan. It came about because the entire generation led by Moses, which knew how to farm in Egypt, had died off after wandering for 40 years in the wilderness. Because the Israelites were nomads and did not know how to do arable farming, they had to depend on the Canaanites to learn how to farm. It seems to have been the Canaanite practice to ensure fertilisation by the practice of having essentially heterosexual men going into the temple of Baal to have intercourse with male prostitutes. The Israelites apparently followed suit, thinking this was just good farming practice. We do not know the course of the practice, but we do know when it started (1451 BC, when the Israelites came into the Promised Land) and when it stopped (639 BC, during the reign of King Josiah just before the Babylonian exile). By Josiah's time, the practice had become so widely accepted in Israel that it had moved from the temples of Baal into the Jewish temple in Jerusalem. This homoerotic practice was probably accepted then as 'standard agricultural practice', in much the same way that homoerotic actions in rugby are accepted today as 'manly sport'; otherwise, it would not have been admitted into the temple in Jerusalem.

According to some scholars, the 'holiness' priests wrote the injunction against this homoerotic practice and then ascribed it to Moses (Snaith, 1975). It was an effective move by the priests. When King Josiah heard the injunction for the first time, he banned such practices in the temple. 'He broke down the houses of the male temple prostitutes that were in the house of the Lord, where the women did weaving for Asherah' (2 Kings 23:7). This socially sanctioned form of homosexuality would have been practiced in some form in Israel for approximately 800 years, which would have included the time of David and Jonathan. It would allow both homosexual and heterosexual men to practice homoerotic behaviour without guilt, and perhaps make it possible for predominately homosexual people to marry wives because homosexual expression could be practiced alongside their heterosexual behaviour. If they were unable to impregnate their wives, their brothers could do so after their death, and the resulting child would bear its mother's dead husband's name.

There are several comments or questions that could be raised about this practice. One would be, 'Of course they should have thrown this abominable practice out.' Another would be, 'Why was the practice so acceptable to the priests and society that they would have admitted it into the temple in the first place? What did it contribute to society that sanctioned its practice for nearly 800 years in places of worship?'

Families of Choice

The most powerful religious taboo with which the Church is wrestling at the moment concerns homosexuality, so let us see how the taboo about homosexuality can be turned on its head. The preconceived notion that homosexuality is sinful seems to be blocking a spiritual covenant. In order to understand this we have to reflect on the nature of families.

We all have a family of origin, but we also have a family of choice. If all goes naturally, we lose our family of origin; our parents die before we do, and our brothers and sisters move away to form their own families. We all therefore need a family of choice to replace our naturally-diminishing family of origin. Christianity makes the family important, particularly the family of choice, rather than marriage. Recently, the concept of marriage has tended to replace that of family, as if the two were identical. A close look at Scripture indicates that family is important and that marriage may be of lesser importance than the family. Marriages are temporary and time-limited, but families can go on even after marriage is extinguished by the death of the couple. St Paul writes: 'If anyone thinks that he is not behaving properly towards his fiancée, if his passions are strong, and so it has to be, let him marry as he wishes; it is no sin. Let them marry' (1 Cor. 7:36). Jesus also says that there are no marriages in heaven (Luke 20:34). When I was a missionary in Zambia in the

1960s the major debate in the church concerned what to do about tribal chiefs with several wives, who converted to Christianity. The ruling was that upon baptism and confirmation all the wives could come to communion because they had one husband; but the chief was instantly excommunicated because he had more than one wife. The African bishops asked the archbishops in the Anglican Consultative Council to rule that monogamy was not essential to Christianity in these instances. They asked that, upon conversion, because of cultural considerations, the chief could be admitted into communion and keep all of his wives, rather than giving up all but the first one. The archbishops agreed to this request. In making the request that they did, and in getting the response they did from the archbishops, the Anglican Communion implicitly affirmed that being a member of a family is more important than being in a monogamous marriage.

What happens in Scripture if it is not possible to have a family of choice in the usual way of husband meets wife? Consider Naomi and Ruth. When Naomi's husband dies, she and Ruth make a covenant with each other to be a 'chosen family' to each other. This was a covenant made before God between these two women who loved one another: 'Where you go I will go, where you will lodge I will lodge. Your people shall be my people and your God my God. Where you die, I will die – there I will be buried. May the Lord do thus and so to me, and more as well, if even death parts me from you!' (Ruth 1:16–18)

This was a covenant between two people who loved each other of the same gender, and who agreed to be family of choice to each other. It was valued in Scripture and not seen as a threat to the institution of marriage. This covenant did not stop Ruth from marrying Boaz, but then multiple marriages were acceptable in those days. It was an alternative to the usual kind of family of choice that comes about by marriage. Naomi coaches Ruth to have a relationship, and then to marry Boaz, but the child born of that union is given to Naomi to nurse. When the child is given to Naomi, the women who were living there said: ' "A son has been born to Naomi " ' (Ruth 4:17). Note that the child's birth was

linked to Naomi, not to Ruth. The child of these two women's
covenanted relationship was named Obed, the father of Jesse,
and the father of King David. This may have been irregular, but
it was done by covenant before God.

Consider also David and Jonathan. David and Jonathan so
loved each other that Jonathan made David, the man he loved
more than women, a member of his royal family. He not only
gave David his place as successor to the throne of Israel, but said
he would serve David in that role. The impact of this would be
like Prince Charles saying, 'I love a man more than Diana, more
than Camilla, and I give him my rights of succession to the
throne, and will act as his servant when he comes to reign'. The
House of David therefore owed a debt of gratitude to the House
of Jonathan. Both Jesus and the gospel writers seem aware of this
debt of the house of David to the House of Jonathan. They
describe John as the disciple that Jesus (Son of David) loved.
Jesus pays off this debt of honour of his ancestor David by
making John, the disciple that he loved, his chosen family and
next of kin.

In practice, Jesus enters into family of choice same-gender
covenant, both collectively as well as individually. Collectively,
in Luke 22.27–30, Jesus says to his disciples at the Last Supper,
'You are those who have stood by me in my trials; and I confer
on you, just as my Father has conferred on me, a kingdom, so
that you may eat and drink at my table in my kingdom, and you
will sit on thrones judging the twelve tribes of Israel' (Luke
22.28–30). Here Jesus gives the kingdom to his disciples, who
become members of the royal family of David by adoption, not
by blood. This parallels and repays Jonathan's covenant made
with David (1 Sam. 23.17–18) where Jonathan said: ' "Do not be
afraid; for the hand of my father Saul shall not find you; you
shall be king over Israel, and I shall be second to you; my father
Saul also knows that this is so" '.

At the individual level, Jesus makes John, 'the disciple whom
he loved', a chosen member of his immediate family and entrusts
his mother to her new 'son', and son to his new 'mother' from

the cross (John 19:26–7). In this newly created family, John becomes Jesus' next of kin partner, and the primacy of this partnership takes precedence over the traditional responsibilities of Jesus' natural brothers and sisters. Mary goes to live with John after the crucifixion, not with James, as we might expect, who is Mary's next oldest son. James was important and led the church for a brief time after the crucifixion in Jerusalem. Just as David displaced Jonathan in the royal family, so John, Jesus' chosen next of kin, displaces James, Jesus' natural next of kin. Mary acknowledges Jesus' choice of John as his family of choice, by going to live with John, rather than with her son James. John 19:27 records that 'from that hour the disciple took her into his own home'.

All of these demonstrate an underlying principle, which is the transformation of loss and taboo into the raw material of spiritual growth and enlightenment. It is the central spiritual dynamic running through the Old and New Testaments. This dynamic pattern is missed, even inhibited, when our view of what is religious is debased into seeing it merely as superego, and confusing spirituality with what is nice and socially acceptable. If we do this, we become blind to the other spiritual patterns because they do not tissue-match with our preconceptions. Life is anything but 'nice'. Instead it is loving, powerful, transformative, and very unexpected, because it is connected with a living God.

This raises one of the central issues in the church today. If David and Jonathan, Jesus and John, can make same-gender covenants for family of choice, why not gays and lesbians? There is ample scriptural precedent for same-gender covenants before God.

The Sacramental Aspects of Love-Making

Our prejudices may have made us blind to the fact that there may be in fact, not one, but two covenants enacted at the Last Supper. The first was the new Passover meal, but the other was the fulfilment and repayment of the debt which the house of David owed to the House of Jonathan. Jesus actually said: ' "This is my body; this is my blood" ', with John physically lying on his breast. If there were two covenants, might there possibly be three sacraments in the Protestant sense (or eight in the Catholic sense?). The additional sacrament would, for example, arise from Jesus making someone you love, of the same gender, into your family of choice.

This would be different from marriage. However, it is similar to the pattern of transforming the taboo of homosexuality into its highest form, alongside the other transformed taboos that have so nourished the church through the centuries. Because God and his plans are greater than each of us, our own understanding about the way he works may often stop us from seeing the obvious in the way he may be acting in our lives. The idea of a sacrament is that the physical can open the way for the spiritual to come more fully into our lives. Water, oil, bread, and sexual intercourse can be the physical means by which we feel God acting in our lives.

Making people of the same gender into family of choice is carried on in religious communities. We do not often register that monks and nuns regularly make a covenant before God to form themselves into a new family of choice. As such, they put on wedding rings, change their name, and pool their finances, which is what happens in the formation of any new family. We say that they 'marry Jesus', but in common with brides and grooms, their marriage to Jesus is revealed in their relationship with each other. They make their family of choice collectively. That bypasses the taboo that might arise if we saw them doing this as individual couples.

This can be illustrated by a conversation I had with a nun who attended a series of Pastoral Psychology seminars that I taught. The subject on that particular afternoon was sexuality. The nun declared that her religious vows constituted marriage vows to the Lord Jesus Christ. These were, of course, unconsummated by any physical and sexual act, but she hoped that her spiritual marriage to Christ would be consummated in heaven. I suggested that as marriage vows only exist during our mortal life, 'as long as you both shall live,' her marriage, like any marriage, must be consummated in this life. Jesus said there were no marriages in heaven. Might physically receiving the body and blood of her spouse into her at Communion constitute the consummation of her marriage in this life? As males could also go to the altar and physically receive the body and blood of their spouse into them, could this begin a discussion of the ways in which the sacramental aspect of sexuality was non-gender specific? Did a monk also consummate his marriage to the Lord in the same way? If so, could lesbian and gay couples do the same as well, sacramentally?

We went on to reflect that the prefaces of both the Anglican and Roman Catholic marriage services say that the relationship between husband and wife is the same as between Christ and his Church. So, if we compare intercourse with God in Holy Communion to what happens in marriage, the following two points can be deduced?

1) There is a higher purpose in sexual intercourse than procreation, just as there is a higher purpose to Holy Communion than just being physically fed.

2) If we compare sexual intercourse between persons with that between Christ and his Church at Communion, that intercourse on a spiritual or supernatural level is not gender specific (i.e. not just limited to being between male and female).

This view of sexual intercourse as a sacrament is not highly developed because we have inherited the Roman Catholic view that the highest aspect of sexual intercourse is for procreation, together with the couple giving comfort to each other. It is interesting that the Catholic Church would endorse the discipline of fasting, an act which suppresses the natural for a supernatural end, so that receiving Holy Communion is enhanced after a period of abstaining from natural food. However, birth control is considered a sin because it is felt to be unnatural to suppress fertilisation and childbirth; the supernatural aspect of sex is left out of the discussion altogether. Failure to see birth-control as a form of fasting, whereby the bride and groom can give each other the sacrament of sex, is essentially like not seeing the supernatural aspect of marriage.

Conclusion

The purpose of this chapter is not so much to convince, but to open for discussion the idea that God may be following his usual pattern of acting through what we have formerly considered taboo. He did this when he confronted Peter in the book of Acts with the fact that he gave the Holy Spirit to not only the Jews, but also the Gentiles. His injunction to Peter was not to call impure what God has made clean (Acts 10:15). To his credit, Peter overcame a lifetime of training and prejudice concerning Gentiles as outsiders in order to follow God's new revelation.

If God transforms what is spiritual from its opposite, and if self righteousness is addressed by having life turned upside down and finding ourselves wrong-footed, perhaps it is spiritually beneficial to stop thinking of God as always being supportive of our status quo just because he loves us. When God is assumed to think as we do, then we feel justified to attack our enemies in his name. How many wars have been started in the name of God? With God on our side, we begin to see our enemies as less than human.

Instead, if we assume God to be constantly on the opposite side to ourselves, challenging us, then we are less likely to attack. Instead we might find ourselves saying, 'Oh God, why do you always demand that I love and forgive my enemies? I am finding it so very difficult to do just now, especially when my people are under threat'. That would certainly help keep us more focused spiritually.

The pattern of God's action revealed in Scripture is to reverse what is considered taboo. To convert tragedy into victory is the hallmark of the living God. This can be seen in action, not only in Scripture, but also in our own lives. Each one of us will have experienced spiritually transforming events in our lives. The challenge for us is to see how our own taboos have been subverted and resulted in the leading of a healthier and happier life.

7

Jesse W. Abell

INTERPRETIVE PROCESSES

The Evolution of Biblical Studies

While all Christians acknowledge the Bible as the Word of God, we do not always agree on how to interpret it. In fact disagreements about interpreting Scripture were at the heart of the Reformation. Historically the Roman Catholic Church taught that the Bible could only be understood through the tradition of the Church and only with the guidance of the clergy.

Protestants resisted these claims, and the Reformers insisted that the Holy Spirit enabled all people, lay or ordained, to understand the Bible. They argued, and indeed many continue to argue, that the Bible is perspicuous and that there was a 'plain meaning of Scripture' which any reader could grasp by intently reading the biblical text.

The search for the 'plain meaning of Scripture' developed over time into a science of biblical interpretation, called *hermeneutics*. The field of hermeneutics is concerned with the interpretation of the text itself (a process called *exegesis*) as well as the application of the text to contemporary life. In the classic hermeneutical tradition, the aim of the reader is to decipher the original meaning of a passage, the meaning that the author had in mind. In this sense there can be only a single interpretation for a passage, one plain meaning of that Scripture. One has only to discover it through careful study.

Contemporary scholars on the other hand have begun to question whether there is only one meaning for any given passage. For these thinkers it is futile to focus on the search for a single meaning. Moreover some would argue that it is impossible to recover the original intent of the authors. Everything that we do is influenced by our previous experiences and our presuppositions, and modern scholars assert that we can never separate our own experiences and beliefs from those of the text (or the author of the text). Scripture, therefore, takes on a unique meaning for each individual reader.

In the discussion of biblical interpretation, then, there are two important questions to ask. First, is there a single meaning for a passage, or are there multiple, possible meanings? And second, do readers need to separate themselves from the text to allow the passage to speak for itself? The way we answer these questions determines how we approach the Bible and how we go about interpreting it.

These questions have led some scholars to turn their attention to the relationship between the text and the reader. They have recognised that a reader can exercise great influence over the message that is conveyed, and as a result scholars are beginning to examine the various ways the background, experience and thinking of readers have affected their understanding of the Bible. Psychology can offer helpful input into this discussion.

Both psychology and biblical scholarship are important fields for us as Christians of the twenty-first century. As the world becomes more aware of psychological research and theories, the Church increasingly experiences a need for further integration the two fields, but the two disciplines are rather broad and multifaceted, and thus it is essential to develop some sort of framework for studying psychological hermeneutics.

In this essay I am primarily concerned with the insights of

cognitive psychology. These theories have a great deal to offer us as we set out to examine how our own psychology influences the way we read and understand the Bible. Cognitive psychologists already have observed certain patterns and tendencies, some-times called *cognitive biases*, in human thinking. These tendencies also impact the way we interpret a given scriptural passage.

I think it is also important first to mention constructivist theory and its implications for exegetical work. This theory explores the way we interpret and experience every aspect of our daily lives. While constructivism is usually set apart as a school of thought in its own right, it is also a sort of meta-theory that encompasses all other branches of psychology. This theory compliments cog-nitive psychology particularly well and, in Theissen's framework (Theissen, 1987), would probably fit best in the cognitive cate-gory. Insights from constructivism challenge us to reconsider how we encounter the text at each and every reading event.

All of this discussion of psychology and biblical interpretation is not merely some scholastic exercise. It has much to say to the Church today, to all who read the Bible, to you and me in con-temporary society. Just as the observations of cognitive psy-chology and constructivism may be applied to the exegetical process, I would argue that cognitive biases can also apply to our interpretation of Scripture. For each of the biases and theories I introduce, I will provide examples from the gospels to illustrate how that particular issue might be at work when we read and interpret Scripture. It is my hope that by familiarising ourselves with our own tendencies and thinking patterns, we might learn to approach the sacred text in new ways and to take from it a fuller understanding of the Word of God.

A Constructivist Look at Biblical Interpretation

To begin this discussion, we should first consider one of the newer and more radical theories of modern psychology, called *constructivism*. This theory challenges our assumptions about the very nature of reality, the world around us, and even the way we look at Scripture. Those who search for a 'plain meaning of Scripture' do so based on the assumption that in the Biblical text there is a single, objective message, and this assumption is part of a larger worldview in which there is a single, objective reality that all people share and observe. This view of reality underpins most of the way we talk and interact with each other.

Constructivists, however, challenge this worldview, arguing that our reality is not objective at all. Rather it is entirely subjective, and our experiences of events and our perceptions of the world shape our own personal realities. It is entirely possible for two people to go through the same event and yet to have entirely different experiences and perspectives on it.

This concept should not be totally foreign. Take for example the disparity that might exist between the daily experiences of two people, working side-by-side, when one suffers from depression and the other does not. The difference in perceptions can be astounding. It is as though they live in entirely different worlds.

This phenomenon has implications that reach far beyond depression. This interpretative work is a part of each of our lives and every moment of them. Constructivist observations also apply to the world of theology and biblical studies. The mental framework we have created to interpret the world influences everything we think, hear and read. Whether we recognise it or not, each of us perceives the world in our own way, and we uniquely interpret whatever we perceive. Even though all Christians may share the same gospels, we approach the texts with unique expectations. As we read, we make sense of the message according to the cognitive framework we have constructed, and as a result we come to our own unique conclusions.

It is no surprise then that two people reading the same gospels can derive different meanings from them. One illustration of this is our responses to the descriptions of God as Father in the New Testament. Throughout the gospels, Jesus refers to God as his 'heavenly Father.' Take, for instance, Jesus' prayer for the Church in John 17:

> After Jesus had spoken these words, he looked up to heaven and said, 'Father, the hour has come; glorify your Son so that the Son may glorify you, since you have given him authority over all people, to give eternal life to all whom you have given him. And this is eternal life, that they may know you, the only true God, and Jesus Christ whom you have sent. I glorified you on earth by finishing the work that you gave me to do. So now, Father, glorify me in your own presence with the glory that I had in your presence before the world existed.' (v. 1–5)

The language of God as Father is commonplace in the gospel texts, and the prominence of this concept of God as Father is reflected in the Lord's Prayer that so many Christians recite regularly. This language, however, is by no means neutral. Readers will respond to these descriptions according to their past experiences, specifically their experiences with their own fathers.

Those of us who have grown up in households with good and caring fathers will relate intimately with this attribution of God and will see God in similar way, as one who loves, cares, and provides for us. On the other hand, for those who have grown up without the presence of their father this imagery will be flat. Without a personal history involving a father figure, this description of God will be little more than any other label we give to God.

For some, this description will be an obstacle to encountering God in this passage. Although the Father language was no doubt meant to convey God as personal and intimate, it could do just the opposite and alienate readers. Feminist theologians have brought this to our attention. To women who have felt oppressed by male domination, the use of this masculine imagery evokes feelings of marginalisation and conceptualises God as over-bearing and controlling. For these reasons, modern church leaders and scholars have searched for broader, more inclusive descriptions of God.

Worse yet are the emotional and cognitive reactions of those who have had traumatic experiences with their fathers. If readers have grown up in an abusive environment, they might relate to fathers as violent, belligerent figures from their past. The mention of 'Father' could stir up feelings of powerlessness and fear. In church and religious contexts, the use of Father language serves as painful reminders of their abuse history. These men and women often struggle with the traditional phrases and prayers the Church uses because they simply cannot connect to God with such negatively loaded imagery.

It is astounding how these reactions are different from one another. The meaning of 'Our Father' is dependent upon each person's past experience of father figures. Although they are reading the same gospel passage, they will arrive at very different interpretations because their various backgrounds influence how they interpret what they see and hear.

As we go throughout our day, we encounter the world through our senses. On their own the sights, sounds, tastes, and smells are meaningless, for it is the way we define and interpret these stimuli that creates the meaning of our experiences. Kelly, a pioneer in constructivist theory, referred to this as *construing*:

> By construing we mean 'placing an interpretation': a person places an interpretation on what is construed. He erects a structure, within the framework of which the substance takes shape or assumes meaning. The substance which he construes does not produce the structure; the person does. (Kelly, 1991, p. 35)

Constructivists call to us to stop and reconsider what we believe to be the reality around us and to rethink what we believe to be true. The world we have come to know is not as objective as we so often have assumed it is. Everything we encounter and experience becomes what we interpret it to be. Even the little things, the mundane objects of daily life, are cast in a new light.

Kelly is not the only modern thinker to recast reality in this framework. Berger, a sociologist, has written at length about 'the social construction of reality,' especially as it applies to our understanding of religion and the supernatural. He explores how our entire world, our reality, is the product of a deeply held, though largely unexamined, cognitive framework that has been influenced by socialisation processes. Experiences that are realistic only seem realistic because they conform to our conceptions of reality. Similarly supernatural events only appear otherworldly to us because they do not conform to our definitions of what is real. Instead they defy our beliefs about what is natural and worldly, and as a result we believe they are extraordinary and supernatural.

Constructivism has had a significant impact in psychological and academic circles, and many people are recognising the importance of this outlook on human thought and behaviour. Each person is made up of unique experiences, emotions, theories about the world, and thought patterns, and these factors cause everyone to interpret in their own way the events and experiences of the world. This means that the same event can mean different things to different people. The meaning which people create is the culmination of their past experiences, their expectations about the world, their thinking patterns and their social context.

This theory may explain how so many Christian groups can use the same Scriptures and reach entirely different conclusions about God, the Church, salvation and Christian living. A biblical passage does not contain a message waiting to be read, but rather the message is construed as the audience reads the text in light of their experiences, emotions and beliefs. They construct a meaning for the text as they read the words of the Bible. Because each person has a unique history of experiences and beliefs, each will encounter the text in a unique way and will draw out of it a unique interpretation.

Our differing views of salvation demonstrate how the cognitive framework we use can influence the conclusions we reach. Pruyser (1991) wrote that people tend to be attracted to one of three views of the atonement, depending upon the psychological issues at play in their lives. Pruyser, as a student of psychoanalysis, describes these underlying psychological issues in terms of unconscious conflict between the ego, superego, and id. While his descriptions have these conflicts and other psychodynamic assumptions in mind, his observations also demonstrate the constructivist theory. He writes that our view of the atonement is determined by the 'symbol systems' we use and by the purpose, function, motivations and roles that the atonement themes offer us.

Scripture itself does not clarify which of the three views of the atonement – the Ransom Theory, the Satisfaction Theory and the Moral Theory – is best. Indeed there are Scripture passages that could be used to defend each. Supporters of the *Ransom Theory*, who believe that God through Christ has delivered us out of bondage to sin and death, point to Jesus' own words:

> 'whoever wishes to become great among you must be your servant, and whoever wishes to be first among you must be slave of all. For the Son of Man came not to be served but to serve, and *to give his life as a ransom for many*.' (Mark 10:43–5, emphasis mine)

Those who favour the *Satisfaction Theory* also look to the gospels. They believe that by sinning humanity violated divine Law, and that because God is just, God requires satisfaction for these transgressions. Passages like John the Baptist's description of Jesus and the famous verse from John 3.16 suggest that Christ endured suffering and death so that we would not be punished for our sins. John the Baptist once proclaimed about Jesus, ' "Here is the *Lamb* of God who *takes away the sin* of the world!" ' (John 1:29, emphasis mine) John's use of the lamb imagery connotes a sense of sacrifice, like the sin offerings that were offered in the temple.

Likewise advocates of the *Moral Theory* turn to Scripture as the foundation of their view of Jesus as *Christus Victor*. They believe that humanity is created in the image of God but that at the same time humanity is imperfect and falls short of the ideal. Therefore God sent Jesus Christ, who being fully God whilst fully human, could be the perfect human and could set an example for his followers by his life, teachings, and moral uprightness. After all, Jesus instructed his followers to follow his example if they wanted to share in everlasting life:

> 'The one who rejects me and does not receive my word has a judge; on the last day the word that I have spoken will serve as judge, for I have not spoken on my own, but the Father who sent me has himself given me a commandment about what to say and what to speak. *And I know that his commandment is eternal life.* What I speak, therefore, I speak just as the Father has told me.' (John 12:48—50, emphasis mine)

Advocates of these three major views of the atonement can all appeal to Scripture in their defence. So why do they each reach the conclusions they do?

Ultimately they are likely to read the Gospel in light of their own beliefs, experiences, personal needs and wants and their assumptions about themselves, about the world and about God. All of these beliefs and thoughts have caused them to approach the world in a particular way, and in the Gospel they all will find an answer to what they see and experience as the human condition.

Each way of interpreting the Gospel message is inseparably linked to the individual history and the cultural traditions that each reader brings, consciously or unconsciously, to the reading event. The challenge for those studying the Scriptures is to recognise the beliefs and experiences that influence their reading of the biblical text. Once they have become aware of the influence of their expectations and beliefs on their interpretation, they can at least attempt to see the text in a new light, so that the Scriptures become more than reflections of their own presuppositions.

Cognitive Biases and Selective Attention

Constructivism is not the only psychological theory that should be of interest to readers of the Bible. The cognitive school of thought also has a lot to offer. As a result of research and observation, psychologists have discovered common tendencies, termed *biases*, that affect the way humans perceive and process data. While these specific 'cognitive biases' are often applied to human behaviour in daily life and interactions with society, they also have implications for the way we study and interpret Scripture. They can help Christians to understand what presuppositions and expectations they bring to the text and to examine how this cognitive and emotional 'baggage' influences their interpretation of Scripture.

One psychological concept for consideration is *selective attention*, sometimes called 'sensory accommodation'. It is rooted in the awareness that from birth, humans are exposed to a plethora of stimuli. Often the senses are exposed to more input than a person can possibly handle at one time, so as people develop they learn to selectively attend to sensory data. They choose to pay attention to what they believe is the most important data and to filter out the rest.

Recognising and processing stimuli is largely cognitive work. People attend to stimuli that seem most pressing; for instance, when driving an automobile, visual stimuli become the most important, to the neglect of the senses of touch or smell. One's experiences and life history help determine what stimuli will be noticed and processed. Without this adaptation, people would be overwhelmed by information and would be incapable of responding and reacting in their environment. In a similar way, when preoccupied or distracted on a Sunday morning, we may not really be following or listening to the vicar's sermon until a word or phrase or story catches our attention for a reason, perhaps because it is unexpected, seems important, or because it is familiar or meaningful to us.

While selective attention is usually applied to the prioritisation of what our senses detect, selective attention may also be at work in our comprehension of texts, primarily by determining what we notice when we read. Most university students can relate some occasion in which they tried to read a book and were reading the words without really comprehending them. Even though they visually followed very word, paragraph by paragraph, they did not really process the information – until they came to word or phrase that stood out to them and caught their attention. Often that particular phrase or word reminded them of something they had read or heard before or because it was something that stood out as odd.

The same can be said of biblical study. We may be selectively reading the text, heeding its words in some cases while ignoring them in others. This is probably most true in casual reading events. When we read the Scripture text, as is the case with other texts, we tend to notice the things that, for one reason or another, catch our attention. The elements that we notice may be those that we already have been taught to believe are the most important point of the passage. Or, while reading, a word or phrase may jump out at us, perhaps because it is unusual or because we have never noticed it before. In other cases, the words of the biblical author resonate with emotions or ideas that we ourselves bring with us to the text.

In this way new life circumstances and experiences can continually impact the way we read the Bible, even if a passage is very familiar. We may get something different out of the passage each time we read it. This fluid understanding allows the text to be meaningful to us with each reading and makes it timeless and relevant. Though we have heard the Bible's message before, parts of it may seem to be new to us each time we read it.

While learning something new about a passage may be exciting and desirable, it also can be a drawback because readers must give less attention to other parts of the text in order to focus on the new details. Thus one part of the passage is examined while the remainder is overlooked or underappreciated. Some scholars have cautioned to us to avoid enmeshing our past experiences and beliefs with our reading of Scripture because in these cases there is a risk of missing the author's intended message. To read the passage without taking all of it in is to miss some or, in the worst circumstances, most of what the author intended to convey to the audience.

When coming to any biblical text, readers must be careful to take all of the passage in and to process it entirely if they are to fully comprehend the author's message. Often the message is illuminated by the various details the author included in the story. If we miss out on any one of these aspects, we might not fully appreciate the message.

Selective attention can also cause us to gloss over details that may point to deeper, fuller meanings of the gospel story. What we bring with us to the text – be it emotional state, educational training, intent and purpose on the occasion, etc. – influences what we are likely to notice or ignore. In almost every situation that this occurs, we are unaware that we are screening the passage and unconsciously filtering its details. Sometimes the little things, like the author's use of language or a verse's consistency with the rest of the gospels, mean quite a bit. When we miss these important details, our reading of the text can be unfortunate at best and dangerous at worst. One particular example of this is the language used by the evangelists to describe the crowd in the Passion narrative.

Call to mind the part of the story where Jesus stands before Pilate for judgement. You might remember Pilate presenting Jesus to 'the crowd,' or perhaps to 'all the people,' or even to 'the Jews.' All of these phrases are used in the Passion narrative – but not by the same evangelist.

In Mark's gospel, generally considered to be the first written gospel text (*c.* 60 CE), Pilate brings Jesus before the crowd:

> So *the crowd* came and began to ask Pilate to do for them according to his custom. Then he answered them, 'Do you want me to release for you the King of the Jews?' For he realized that it was out of jealousy that the chief priests had

handed him over. But the *chief priests* stirred up *the crowd* to
have him release Barabbas for them instead. (Mark 15:8–11,
emphasis mine)

Mark suggests that Pilate is addressing everyone who is around
the praetorium, and he clearly is saying that the chief priests,
who have long been trying to get rid of Jesus, are turning the
crowd against Jesus.

Matthew and Luke (*c.* 70 – 80 CE) read much the same way, as
is typical of much of the gospel story presented in the Synoptic
gospels. Of course each evangelist adds his own twist. Matthew
also incriminates the elders along with the chief priests in per-
suading the crowd (Matt. 27.20). Luke mentions the scribes and
the chief priests throughout Jesus' trial before Pilate and Herod
(Luke 22:66, 23:13). These elaborations are not surprising as both
Matthew and Luke seem especially concerned about the chief
priests and scribes in their gospels; remember that they both
include Jesus' 'Woes' to the Jewish leaders of that time.

By the time we arrive at the fourth and latest gospel, attributed
to John (*c.* 95 CE), the language has changed entirely. No longer is
it simply 'the crowd' that is indicting Jesus. Now it is 'the Jews'
who seek to crucify Jesus:

From then on Pilate tried to release him, but *the Jews* cried
out, 'If you release this man, you are no friend of the
emperor. Everyone who claims to be a king sets himself
against the emperor. (John 19:12, emphasis mine)

The label of 'the Jews' is powerful and reminiscent of language
used elsewhere, particularly the phrase 'for fear of the Jews'.
Earlier in John's gospel, Herod is upset by the teaching of John
the Baptist but does not murder him right away 'for fear of the
Jews' (John 7:13). Similarly after Jesus is crucified, the disciples
are terrified and hide themselves away 'for fear of the Jews'
(John 20:19).

To be sure, there is a reason for this use of language. John obviously is not anti-Semitic; after all, he is Jewish. Rather this language follows the development of the first Christian community: it reveals the estrangement between the followers of Jesus and the rest of the Jewish community. At first Christians were simply a group of Jews who embraced Jesus of Nazareth as the Messiah. As time passed, however, the differences between those who believed Jesus was the Messiah and those who did not became increasingly prominent. By the time John writes his gospel the two groups have clarified their identities, and Christians are no longer just one of many sects within Judaism. They now have established themselves as a separate and unique religious group.

The differences in language in the Passion narratives are striking, but how many of us would notice the variation if we were not already on the lookout for it? Generally readers do not take notice of particular language used until they are informed about it – unless they have other motives for noticing language usage. In the past discrimination has been justified and hatred enflamed using some of this very language, taken out of its literary and historical context. Word choice might seem a small matter to some, but we must never forget that it can have serious ramifications.

If we as Christians seriously embrace the Scriptures as the rule of faith, then we should also seek to understand them as fully as possible. Fortunately most churches and religious groups encourage their members to read the biblical text as a whole and to avoid selectively using the text, but it is all too easy to gloss over details or to focus on the passages we agree with and to dismiss those with which we have problems. By picking and choosing what passages to use and which not to use, readers reach unbalanced and inaccurate conclusions regarding the biblical message.

While most Christians frown upon selective use of the Bible to further one's own agenda, research suggests that readers have an overwhelming tendency to do just that. Psychologists have observed that people tend to cling to the beliefs they hold, even if it seems that their beliefs are unreasonable. In fact research shows that when confronted with information people tend to attend only to the data that confirm their beliefs, all the while ignoring evidence to the contrary. This phenomenon is known as *confirmation bias*, or 'belief bias'.

Confirmation bias is already a recognised obstacle in research studies, because investigators have a tendency to conduct research in order to validate pre-existing opinions rather than impartially seeking results. For this reason it is recommended that researchers collaborate with others who disagree with their hypotheses. Confirmation bias is also an important concern of the medical field, which cautions doctors and clinicians to carefully consider all the symptoms of a patient when forming a diagnosis because helping professionals have a tendency to form a premature conclusion and then to look only for those symptoms which confirm that diagnosis, rather than thoroughly considering the presenting problem with all its symptoms and then forming a conclusion.

This tendency should also be a concern for biblical scholars and all readers of the Bible. When faced with a controversial issue, readers will, consciously or unconsciously, tend to seek out passages that resonate with their views while passing over other, less agreeable passages.

For instance, in the debate on the nature of hell, advocates of the existence of a place of eternal punishment will gravitate towards passages like ' "If your hand or your foot causes you to stumble, cut it off and throw it away; it is better for you to enter life maimed or lame than to have two hands or two feet and to be thrown into the eternal fire" ' (Matt. 18:8) or ' "And these will go away into eternal punishment, but the righteous into eternal life" ' (Matt. 25:46). To the contrary, universalist Christians will find particularly important those passages which emphasise the inclusiveness of redemption in Christ, such as ' "And I, when I am lifted up from the earth, will draw all people to myself" ' (John 12:32) and 'The next day [John] saw Jesus coming towards him and declared, "Here is the Lamb of God who takes away the

sin of the world!"' (John 1:29). Still others who favour an anni-
hilist view will concentrate on those passages which speak of a
final end for the souls of the unsaved, such as Jesus' comparison
of hell to the rubbish yard called Gehenna (as in Mark 9.45, 47)
and comparison of eternal death to damnation, like ' "I told you
that you would die in your sins, for you will die in your sins
unless you believe that I am he"' (John 8:24).

It has been said that one can prove nearly anything using the
Bible. This is especially true when passages are taken out of
context and considered apart from the rest of the surround
content or from other passages on the same topic, particularly
those verses that present a conflicting opinion. John Chrysostom,
as well as many other theologians and scholars, was right to say
that the Bible should be considered as a whole. To do this,
however, earnest readers must be careful to consider passages in
their proper contexts, if they want to minimise the influence of
confirmation bias has on their interpretations.

In addition to selective reading and confirmation bias, Christian readers are also influenced by their previous experiences,
from which they form expectations and beliefs about the way the
world operates. As we grow and develop, we create mental
paradigms, or *schemas*, for the various situations that we
encounter in life. Because human beings are constantly exposed
to a plethora of stimuli, we must constantly process all this new
data according to existing schemas. This cognitive processing
technique allows an individual to make sense of what has
occurred and to categorise it according to a cognitive framework
developed and maintained by previous experiences and learning. Schemas help us to anticipate things that happen in the
world, and they enable us to process our experiences more
quickly and efficiently. Without them, the stimuli we take in
would be cognitively overwhelming.

Presuppositions and Cognitive Dissonance

Although they are often beneficial, schemas can also create internal conflict and can affect how we see ourselves and the world. At times our experiences or our behaviour seems to contradict previously held beliefs and schemas. This tension threatens our internal stability and our cognitive well-being, which is greatly affected by the consistency with which events are processed. Thus when an experience contradicts our previously held beliefs, uneasiness results. Festinger coined the term *cognitive dissonance* for this feeling of unease.

One of the common manifestations of cognitive dissonance is when an individual's behaviour begins to oppose previously held beliefs or standards. Research on this phenomenon shows that when people's actions clash with their beliefs, they tend not to change their behaviour but to modify their beliefs to accommodate that behaviour. This is important for Christians who rely on Scripture as a guide for standards of conduct. Scripture often provides clear prescriptions for how believers should live their lives, and rarely does one live perfectly in accord with those expectations. At some point believers will be confronted with a situation in which they behave less than perfectly, falling short of the standards set by the Bible. As a result cognitive dissonance is likely to occur. When our behaviour does not conform to biblical standards, we may very well modify our interpretations of the pertinent Scriptures to accommodate our behaviour.

One example is the interpretative approaches to the New Testament teaching on divorce. Jewish leaders of that day permitted a man to divorce his wife provided a certificate of divorce was granted to the woman. To the contrary Jesus teaches his followers that divorce for any reason other than adultery is sinful. In Matthew's gospel, he says:

> It was also said, 'Whoever divorces his wife, let him give her a certificate of divorce.' But I say to you that anyone who divorces his wife, except on the ground of unchastity,

> causes her to commit adultery; and whoever marries a
> divorced woman commits adultery. (5:31–2)

A number of mainline denominations, including the Roman
Catholic Church and the Church of England, uphold this traditional understanding of the permanence of marriage. Many
Christians who are single or married for the first time also have
no problem accepting this prohibition on divorce, but when a
Christian marriage meets its unfortunate end in divorce, the
parties involved must grapple with this passage and its implications for their situation. They very likely will experience cognitive dissonance and will tend to seek alternative explanations of
Jesus teaching, particularly ones which do not conflict with their
actions.

Learning from Our Cognitive Tendencies

Some Christians may find much of this essay troubling, maybe
even offensive. After all, based on what I have said about these
psychological concepts, one might conclude that all Scripture is
entirely subjective, that there are no absolutes and that we can
never know what is true. I think such conclusions would be
erroneous, and I certainly am not trying to argue for this extreme
position. At the same time it would be a mistake to take the other
extreme, arguing that there is one obvious and indisputable
meaning of Scripture or to argue that we can approach the Bible
without being the least bit influenced by our past experiences
and our personalities.

In light of research and our own personal experiences, we
must realise that when we come to the text we bring all that we
are. We read the words of the gospels through the lens of our
lives. We are never entirely objective, no matter how hard we try.
Every interpretation we make will say as much about us as it will
about the text upon which it is based.

Those of us who have been taught to take a phenomenological
approach to exegesis may be discouraged. Scholars and

professors are to be commended for insisting that we should let the text speak for itself without any outside influences, and the Bible as the Word of God certainly deserves such respect and integrity. Yet we must be realistic and acknowledge that our experiences, our situations, recent events, emotions and numerous other factors will influence how the text speaks to us and what we make of its message.

This is not necessarily a bad thing. It is this ever-changing and evolving perspective that brings Scripture to life. As we grow and develop, we will continue to discover new insights and lessons in the biblical text. With each meaningful life event we will encounter the sacred text in a new and fresh way. Passages once taken for granted may evoke feelings of comfort or safety or trust, just at the exact moment that we need to be reassured. Verses we thought we knew fully will suddenly relate intimately to the most important aspects of our lives. The Word of God will continue to take on a new meaning for us. All because God has created us so wondrously that Scripture continues to speak to us throughout the lifespan.

This realisation should prompt us to reflect on exactly what influences our interpretation. While our emotional and cognitive state of mind may help us to see new things in the text, it may also lead us to skew the meaning of the words that God is speaking. We may allow our biases, consciously or subconsciously, to distort the message, but if we are careful, we can also minimise the impact our biases have on our interpretations.

While constructivism teaches us that it is impossible for our perspectives and experiences not to influence the meaning of a passage, other cognitive factors can be controlled or minimised. Issues like selective reading can be largely avoided if we are intent on reading a passage in its fullness. By devoting ourselves to the careful and serious study of the text, as biblical scholars instruct us to do, we can give due consideration to each of the author's writing and allow God the opportunity to speak to us through words or phrases that we might otherwise pass over.

Similarly, when researching or discussing a particular issue, we should not seek out only those passages of Scripture that affirm what we already believe. This is an especially important point for preachers. Among churches where the pastor or vicar chooses the biblical text and topic for sermons, there is a tendency to preach on passages we like and with which we are comfortable. There is also a propensity to ignore difficult passages, like Jesus' harsh words to one of his grieving followers who wanted to go to a family member's funeral: ' "Follow me, and let the dead bury their own dead" ' (Matt. 8:22). It is so easy to avoid passages in the gospels which we have trouble teaching or even accepting ourselves, such as ' "Whoever comes to me and does not hate father and mother, wife and children, brothers and sisters, yes, and even life itself, cannot be my disciple" ' (Luke 14:26). If, however, the entire Bible is inspired by God then church leaders cannot dismiss some of God's Word while selectively promoting other passages.

Indeed, often God speaks to us most powerfully through these difficult passages. We must consider and even wrestle with those passages of Scripture we find most difficult. Using a lectionary that prescribes the texts for each service can be helpful in this regard, but those who do not use a lectionary must be careful to avoid falling into the snare of confirmation bias.

It follows that when confronted with challenging passages, we as Christians are called to conform more and more to the likeness of Christ. Whenever the sacred text calls our attention to some aspect of our lives that needs reforming, we should be open to its wisdom. Our human nature is compelled to rationalise our behaviour and to make excuses for it or to explain the incriminating verses away. If we make ourselves aware of cognitive dissonance and its effect on our thinking, we can be on guard against these tendencies.

This discussion of cognitive dissonance, selective attention, and confirmation bias demonstrates that psychology can inform our theology and our methods of biblical study. Even though we approach God and Scripture as Christians and spiritual beings, we do not stop being humans, and psychology can help us learn more about ourselves as human beings. Perhaps the most important point to take away from this discussion is the real-isation that every interpretation of Scripture is unique, even if only in subtle ways. We all bring different histories and per-spectives to our reading of the text, and as a result each of us will appreciate it in a unique way. If we consider the insights psy-chology has to offer, we should reconsider our approaches to differing interpretations of Scripture.

At the end of the day, these insights should challenge us to be open to the thoughts of others and the meaning that Scripture holds for them. Too, we should be less dogmatic about the interpretation we hold. Rather than insisting that one meaning must be right and all others wrong, we should allow God the freedom to speak to us through the biblical text in various ways, and we should be open to the meanings that our brothers and sisters in faith have to share. Only then can we allow the sacred Scriptures to be all that they were meant to be: the very Word of God.

8
James M. Day

PERSONAL DEVELOPMENT

Introduction

Most of us of have had an experience of being confronted by questions of continuity and change in our identity, our ways of doing things, and our ways of making meaning in life. Consider the familiar experience of looking in the mirror, and being struck that one is at once the same as before, and quite different; different from the day before and different from the person one was years ago, yet recognizably the same person. The mirror might be metaphorical: we might consider ourselves in light of a conversation with a friend who has known us well over time, and be struck by this same paradox. How are continuity and change related in ourselves, in others, and in the very processes of human aging and growth? For many of us, these questions bring to mind the moments and periods of consequential transition through which we have emerged. Consequently we experience life rather differently; our perspectives on ourselves, on others, and the world, had undergone changes.

These fundamental and deeply human questions of continuity and change across the life cycle are the building blocks of developmental psychology. For many people, religion and religious experience are directly implicated in these questions of identity and meaning; when a shift in any domain of experience occurs, it bears also on religious understandings and sensibilities. Some individuals have a keen sense of their religious development awareness of the ways in which their religious faith and practice have developed over time. For many Christians, such changes have an impact on their understanding of Jesus and their ways of reading the gospels.

It should not be surprising, then, that an enduring question in the science of developmental psychology has been whether religious development could be studied alongside and in relation to other features of psychological functioning, such as moral, intellectual, emotional, and aesthetic developments, identity formation, and so on. Formal investigations of religious development have been pursued for a quarter of a century, with varying degrees of theoretical and empirical rigour. Currently there exists a wealth of information, and hundreds of formal investigations which address religious development and how it might be related to other domains of human growth and change.

In this chapter we will consider the basic features of the psychology of religious development, and some of their implications for reading the gospels. We will begin with a broad overview of the relevant scientific literature for two purposes. First, we hope this will be a helpful exercise to illuminate how psychological variables in religious development might affect the way people read the gospels. Second, we hope this will reveal whether people perceive any personal development in the life, activity, and teachings of Jesus, and if so, how they regard such development. We will briefly consider three important domains of theory and research which have contributed to our understanding of religious development: cognitive developmental models; models drawing from the theory of attachment, and narrative models.

After we have outlined the important domains of theory and research in developmental psychology, we will shift attention to their possible consequences for reading Scripture and considering the life and teaching of Jesus. The first set of these consequences concerns the act of reading and suggest that, according to theoretical perspectives and empirical evidence in psychology, people will read the Scriptures and consider the life and teaching of Jesus in synchrony with their level, or stage, of psychological religious development, or according to their style of appropriation of what they deem significant in keeping with the trajectories of their developmental history. The second set of these consequences considers whether, on psychological grounds, readers of the gospels are likely to view development occurring within the life and vocation of Jesus, in the record we have of that in the gospels. This second set of consequences asks whether, on psychological grounds, we are more or less likely to view Jesus, himself, as developing, as we read about him in the biblical record. Finally, returning to questions rooted in the discipline of developmental psychology itself, some prospects for further exploration are proposed.

Several recent reviews of the literature in the psychological study of religious behaviour contain careful theoretical reflection and empirical research, offering perspectives on religious development across the lifespan (e.g. Day, 2001; Day and Youngman, 2003; Saroglou, 2001; Spilka *et al*, 2003). These reviews illustrate many ways in which psychologists have sought to understand religious development. Some focus on the characteristic features of religious experience in specific periods in the life course (e.g. ideas of God in childhood, adolescence, or young adulthood contrasted with later adulthood). Others focus more specifically on particular models of religious development that have a strong record of theoretical interest, conceptual rigour, and empirical research, seeking to clarify concepts and test hypotheses drawn from theory.

Cognitive-Developmental Approaches

The cognitive-developmental model is grounded in the theoretical framework of Jean Piaget, who has made enormous contributions to our understanding of how intellectual functioning not only changes, but develops over the life course in an orderly way. This has been the dominant model in the psychological study of religious development for twenty-five years, influencing clinical practice, religious education, and training of lay and ordained ministers, so we will devote considerable attention to it here.

Piaget advanced the perception of human beings as *epistemic subjects* who are motivated chiefly by the need to make sense of their experiences, even from the very beginning of the lifespan. In this process of sense-making, humans both actively shape and are shaped by their environments. Using their experiences, they establish patterns of thinking about the world, known as schemas, which are used to evaluate and make sense of what is happening in their lives. Experiences that 'fit' into these patterns make sense, and reinforce the schemas. Experiences that do not 'fit', however, create a sense of dissonance between reality and people's understanding of it.

All human experiences are used to revise and reformulate their understanding of what they and their world(s) are like. As their age increases and their biological capacities develop, humans come in contact with stimuli of increasing number and complexity. As a result, humans can actively construct increasingly comprehensive and complex modes of understanding. According to Piaget, these increasingly sophisticated modes of sense-making are constructed in an invariant sequence and hierarchy of stages ordered by deep structures which apply to all cognitive functioning at any given stage. To understand how a person thinks about an event or a problem, we would want to appreciate the specific stage structure that characterises the person's cognitive functioning. This allows us to enter into his or her world of sense-making and invites the person's further development toward the realisation of his or her maximal potential. Piaget's work has influenced our appreciation of intellectual development across the lifespan in every conceivable domain of intellectual functioning and has hugely impacted teaching and assessment practices intellectual development in children. Several of the more significant scholars and practitioners interested in the psychology of religious development have, to varying degrees, embraced Piaget's basic concepts and methods in studying religious development, and have explored its relationship to other domains of human growth and change (such as intellectual, emotional, moral, and aesthetic developments) across the life cycle.

Several researchers have sought to test the notion that development in religious concepts would be closely related to the kind of cognitive development Piaget described (e.g. Batson *et al.*, 1993; Degelman *et al.*, 1984; Elkind, 1964; Goldman, 1964; Peatling and Labbs, 1975; Tamminen and Nurmi, 1995). Their research has found indeed that as capacity for abstraction and complex thinking develop in other areas of thought, so do specific ways in which children think about religious concepts (e.g. God, prayer, and suffering).

Closely following Piaget's work, Lawrence Kohlberg developed Piaget's model of moral judgement development into an elaborate framework of six stages, and related programmes for moral judgement development and moral education. Kohlberg asserted that because religious sense-making includes reflection on moral questions, religious development would be closely linked to moral judgement development. Any 'upward' advancement in moral judgement stages would be likely to stimulate development in religious judgement or faith development. Researchers in the psychology of religious development, such as Fritz Oser, Helmut Reich, and James Fowler incorporated these assumptions into their models of religious development (Fowler, 1981, 1994; Oser and Reich, 1996).

In their research, Oser and Reich (1996) focus on *religious judgement development*. They assume that all people ask existential questions such as 'Why am I here?' 'For what was I made?' 'What is the most interesting, or noble, or worthy, end-point of my life project?' 'What did God intend in creating the world and me?' 'What is the ultimate purpose of life and of my own particular life in relationship to other persons, the natural world, and God?' These questions consider the relationship between the individual person's life and an ultimate being, the world and universe, and his or her ultimate purpose and meaning in life. According to Oser, such questions are integral to human living and to the ends that any and every facet of development might serve. Moreover, these basic questions are pregnant with themes that recur in every epoch of human striving for meaning: freedom, hope, transcendence, time and eternity.

Initiated by his work with Swiss children, adolescents, and adults, Oser has proposed a five-stage model of religious development. In this model, the individual moves from a stage of *heteronomy*, with God as the sole active agent and human beings in a reactive role, through stages of increasing human autonomy and responsibility in relationship to God and for the world. The goal is to reach a stage of *mature religious judgement*, at which the individual has a deep sense of relationship with God and experiences the divine as present everywhere and in all things. Concurrently, the individual also feels a deep sense of solidarity with other human beings and is prompted to live in an attitude of gratitude, and with responsibility for others as well as for themselves. For Oser, this movement from heteronomy to autonomy is stimulated by development in other domains of cognition. It mirrors the movement toward what Piaget called *formal operations* and, in the paradigm of moral judgement development proposed by Kohlberg, the development of per-spective-taking in his conception of mature moral functioning.

James Fowler has studied religious development in a frame-work he calls *faith development*. Like Oser, Fowler also envisages development as a move from a heteronomous stage (called *intuitive-projective faith*), in which one's experience is dominated by feeling the presence of a menacing or protective power, to a stage of autonomous faith (called *universalising faith*). In this final stage individual behaviour is characterised by detached yet compassionate action; the person is capable of moving beyond polarities and can stand outside of one's own tradition without feeling threatened. In Fowler's model, the stages through which one progresses are well-defined, and development is seen as a movement away from dependence on things that have suffused and surrounded one in childhood to a greater capacity for complexity, perspective, role-taking, and universal connection with the divine (Day, 2002; Day and Youngman, 2003; Fowler, 1981, 1994). Fowler's model has greatly impacted religious education, training for lay and ordained ministry, and the bringing of the study of religious development into the main-stream of developmental psychology, more so than any other model of religious development. Many people who read Fow-ler's works recognise themselves in what is being said, thus making the model personally salient even with all its theoretical depth and empirical rigour.

Recent research suggests that moral reasoning, as we have described it in Piaget's and Kohlberg's research, and religious judgement, as Oser *et al.* defined it, help understand how people use religious elements in moral problem-solving, how they understand their own religious experience, and whether or not there is *development* in their religious traditions and in religious personalities who are important in those traditions. Our studies of 500 religiously committed adolescents and young adults in Belgium and England, from Roman Catholic, Anglican, and Islamic faith involvements, showed that there were direct cor-relations between moral judgement, religious judgement and descriptions of religion, religious texts, and whether or not people felt Jesus and Mohammed developed during the course of their respective lives and ministries. After asking our subjects to complete standardised questionnaires so as to assess their moral and religious judgement levels, we asked them to describe a real moral dilemma from their lives, asked them to say whether and how religion played a role in resolving their dilemma, and asked them to respond to the following question: 'In your view, did Jesus/Mohammed *develop* during his lifetime? Would Jesus' own understanding of moral situations have *developed* in the course of his life and ministry? If so, how?' (Day, 2006a, 2006b, in press).

Young people on the lower end of the developmental stage sequences laid out by Kohlberg, Oser, *et al.*, saw religious truth and tradition as fixed, necessarily unchanging, and as dictating moral norms. Our Christian young people in the lower stages (one and two) felt that Jesus developed only chronologically. Typical responses went something like this: 'Jesus was already God when he was born, and even as a baby that meant he was wise and all knowing. He matured physically as we do, but he didn't really need to mature because the fullness of God was in him already, right from the start'; 'Jesus didn't really need to develop in his understanding of moral situations, because he had the understanding of God. His understanding was perfect, and so he wouldn't really have a dilemma. If we are close to God we will see things clearly, and if we follow the Bible we will do the right thing. Jesus was God and he already understood everything, so he automatically knew what to do'.

In contrast, people at the higher end of moral and religious judgement levels in our sample clearly thought Jesus did develop emotionally and psychologically, growing in wisdom, insight, and appreciation of his own ministry. The following examples show something of the contrast between these young people and those with lower scores in moral and religious judgement:

> Jesus developed because that was part of his task. He was of God, and he was God, yet he was fully part of the human experience. If he was to understand our life he had to know something of the whole process of growth in human life, even going through its difficulties and adventures himself. This meant he probably grew not only in just growing up, but in how he understood things, as well.

You can see in the gospels how Jesus is confronted with situations in which he doesn't, at first, know clearly what to do. He has to ponder over things, and then decide, and has difficulty doing so. You get the sense he knew frustration, and perplexity, and that he was growing in facing and working through these things. Maybe he had to go through these things not only to understand the complexity of our situation, but also his own, and to mature into what his ministry was to become. He wasn't, like, just complete, from the beginning. He had to become himself, and to become means to develop.

Clearly, moral and religious reasoning, as they are measured in terms of psychological development, matter in the way people perceive Jesus and read the gospels.

The theory of attachment

We have seen that Fowler's model of faith development acknowledges the importance of affective 'presences' in early religious development. Our early life experience and the importance of emotions experienced at that time can fund our religious understanding with powerful affective components. Whether God first seems to us more menacing than protective, for example, is something that can be important in working out the trajectory of our own development, and can influence our choice of religious group or practice to which we become attracted. Many of us who work with individuals in clinical and pastoral frameworks are aware of how influential such 'primary states' can be, even to the most cognitively sophisticated person, in the understanding of religion, experience of God, and deci-sions-making in life. Another domain of psychological research that has had enormous consequences for understanding the extent to which early emotional experience affects development and religious experience over the course of the lifespan is cent-ered in the theory of attachment.

The theory of attachment has its roots in the work of John Bowlby, who observed close parallels between the quality of early relationships between infants and their parents (especially with mothers), and coping strategies employed by children to deal with the basic challenges of living: how to feel about oneself, how to form relationships with others, and how it would be to experience relationship, satisfaction in school, work, friendship, and love. Bowlby observed a strong relationship between optimal care (in which constancy, loving regard, holding and warm physical contact were primary) in healthy psychological development, and better medical health. Bolstered by additional observations and experimental work of Mary Ainsworth, attachment theory has become one of the most consequential bodies of psychological work, generating many of today's research studies and practices in infant care and child-rearing. One of the most significant aspects of this model is that it has charted the long-term consequences resulting from the quality of relationships during infancy. For example, children who experienced secure relationships in their infancy are more likely to, throughout their life course, have better physical health, more satisfying work, friendship, romantic relationships, have higher test scores for intellectual achievement, and be more loving parents to their own children. On the other hand, children who experienced insecure, ambivalent or anxious-avoidant relationships in their infancy have greater difficulty establishing self-esteem and satisfying relationships in even the most basic (and hugely consequential) facets of living (Ainsworth, 1982; Bowlby, 1969, 1980).

Kirkpatrick, Saroglou, Shaver, and others have recently studied connections between attachment styles and religious experience. They have observed that some people use religion and God in a *compensatory* way, as if to make up for what was absent in human relationships (see also Granqvist, 2002; Kirkpatrick, 1997; Kirkpatrick and Shaver, 1990). Others have observed that people tend to view God through the lens of their early attachment experience. God may be seen as capricious and judgemental or generous and forgiving, according to the relationship patterns established early on in life, and these patterns are difficult to shed or change later on in life. Insecure attachment styles have also been linked to greater likelihood to have an important conversion experience, and to be a part of religious traditions that emphasise law-abidance, group influence and authority, and sectarian functioning (Saroglou, 2001; Spilka *et al.*, 2003; Spilka and Malony, 1991).

Narrative Models of Religious Development

Research in 'narrative psychology' departs from the simple observation that when people talk about life experience and religious experience, they do so in *story form*. People do not simply document their experiences; instead, experiences are fleshed out over time and in context, in the form of *narratives*. Kenneth Gergen (1994) calls narratives 'forms of intelligibility that furnish accounts of events across time. Individual actions [...] gain their significance from the way in which they are embedded within the narrative' (p. 224). According to Gergen, narratives have the following characteristics: (1) an established, valued, endpoint; (2) events recounted are relevant to and serve the endpoint; (3) events are temporally ordered; (4) its characters have a continuous and coherent identity across time; (5) events are causally linked and serve to explain the outcome; and (6) the story has a beginning and an end. The use of narratives as a way of understanding religious experience has been explored by several researchers. Ruard Ganzevoort, for example, has studied how narrative functions in the recovery of men from sexual abuse, and more particularly how their views and understandings of God shift as they elaborate narrative accounts of their experiences (Ganzevoort, 1998a, 1998b). One of Fowler's pupils, Heinz Streib, has shown that understanding narrative facets of religious experience may help us appreciate just how much cognitive styles and developmental stages come to characterise our perception of ourselves, others, religious experience, religious groups, and God. Although Streib was particularly interested in current or former members of fundamentalist and sectarian groups, his work is nevertheless pertinent to a general re-evaluation of stage theory, especially that of Fowler's (Streib, 1991, 1997). Ganzevoot and Streib's appreciation of the narrative self leads us to view the 'self' as *multivocal*. The way one describes oneself, the world, God, and religious experience is in part a function of the *audience* to which one is speaking. Rather than seeing development as within a person, a narrative approach would consider development within the surrounding relationships. The inclusion of a social component in religious development could have considerable consequences for religious education, pastoral practice, and training in psychology and pastoral theology (Day, 1993, 2001, 2002; Day and Naedts, 1999; Day and Tappan, 1996; Day and Youngman, 2003). This work has called for greater sensitivity to social factors such as gender, culture, and religious affiliation when describing religious development, and how religious elements become appropriated in critical life decisions. We have found that adolescent boys and girls, and young adult women and men, talk differently about religious experience, definitions of religion, and religious decision-making. One study showed that young people in Belgium and in England spoke differently about decisions concerning moral dilemmas, and these differences were attributed to their religious affiliation, cultural background, and degree of relative integration or alienation from dominant cultural contexts (Day, 2000, in press)

The Psychology of Religious Development: A Brief Summary

As we said at the outset, it lies beyond the scope of this piece to furnish a complete accounting for all of that developmental psychology has and/or might contribute to our understanding of religious development. We have, however, shown that psychology can help us to understand how development in cognition can influence our understanding of the self, world, religion, and God. We have seen close links between moral development and religious development in several research models. Our appreciation of cognitive complexity and its role in religiosity has been complemented with attention to emotional states and affective development. We have demonstrated how early development, even in the first weeks and months of life, can shape our experience of God and our tendency to gravitate toward or away from religious attitudes and practices much later in life. We now move onto placing these theories alongside our understanding of the gospels.

Jesus and the Gospels: A Psychological View?

Before exploring how the psychology of religious development might offer something for our appreciation of Jesus and the gospels, a couple of caveats are in order. First, we should avoid the temptation to reduce Jesus and the gospels to a mere extension of what psychology can see, study, ask, or document. Religion is studied by people from many scientific points of view, and even within psychology there are many strands and standpoints. Religion also stands beyond what any one science or group of scientific disciplines can say about it, since it takes up the most fundamental questions of human well-being, meaning, purpose, history, nature and the universe. A second danger would be to theologise psychology, or making it psychology's task to obey, mimic, or substantiate the claims of religion or of a particular religious tradition. When we work at the interface of science and religion, we should always try to avoid these pitfalls. Any of us who work across the borders or at the interface of these two domains will agree that avoiding such pitfalls is an important and complex part of our work.

Still, even the most prudent of researchers working at the interface of roles in psychology and religion would affirm that psychological development has a clear impact on how people perceive Jesus and upon how they read the gospels. With an enhanced capacity for appreciating complexity in moral and religious situations, and where an experience of trust in healthy attachments has been consistently present, people structure their own narratives of self and perceive Jesus and the gospels in developmental terms. It seems increasingly logical to people whose own psychological development is enhanced to consider the prospect that Jesus himself developed, and that the gospels represent the unfolding drama of people of faith developing in relationship with God. However, when people are not psychologically developed, their interpretation of moral and religious situations is limited by narrow capacities for decision and judgement, and when this is compounded by a profound experience of mistrust, the notion of development in Jesus' life or in the gospels is seen as contradictory, even heretical. These differences may have considerable implications for ministry, parish life, even doctrinal debates.

Historical, Theological, and Biblical Perspectives

Even as we voice these caveats and attempt to avoid facile reductions of psychology to religion or religion to psychology, we can say some things about how the psychology of human development has occupied an important place in the apostolic and catholic traditions of the Church and its importance to theologians. Perhaps we may be able to say that certain features of the psychology of human development may help us to better appreciate the life and teachings of Jesus as recorded in the gospels.

One of the strong biblical imperatives is that the vocation of every Christian, every person of God, is to grow from image to likeness. This very notion of growing from something into something implies development; it is not simple evolution, but transformation. In the Christian tradition this has been expressed in a variety of ways, describing human development as a move from alienation to relationship with God, from sinfulness to holiness, from being lost to being saved, from emptiness to fulfilment, from rebellion to obedience, from partial to fuller appreciation of the majesty, grace, and loving kindness of God. We are told that in our relationship with God there will be barren periods and fertile periods; times of trial and times of flourishing; times of anger and conflict, and times of continuity and hope. Our life in and with God is one in which we come to know ourselves and others in processes of transformation. This is present from the earliest books in the Bible right through to its last words. There is a powerful and dynamic element to the notion of being in motion as we grow in and with God.

In narrative after narrative, the Bible sets out living accounts of those who have moved through such trajectories of faith intertwined with critical moments in their life development. The Bible shows how Jesus interacts with people in ways that challenge their current stagnation in life while inviting them into a richer, fuller, horizon of imagination about what they might become. Over the history of Christianity, theologians in every major Christian group have addressed the question of human development in relationship to religious development, and the tradition of spiritual direction in the Church is rooted in the notion of human life as a journey from and toward God, in relationship with others. Growth is our very vocation in God. Consider, for example, the following passage from St Paul's letter to the Ephesians:

> It was he who gave some to be apostles, some to be prophets, some to be evangelists, and some to be pastors and teachers, to prepare God's people for works of service, so that the body of Christ may be built up until we all reach unity in the faith and in the knowledge of the Son of God and become mature, attaining to the whole measure of the fullness of Christ. Then we will no longer be infants, tossed back and forth by the waves, and blown here and there by every wind of teaching and by the cunning and craftiness of men in their deceitful scheming. Instead, speaking the truth in love, we will in all things grow up into him who is

the Head, that is, Christ. From him the whole body, joined and held together by every supporting ligament, grows and builds itself up in love, as each part does its work. (4:11–16, NIV)

In this passage St Paul seeks to address what he considers to be the very heart of the Christian life, what the Church is for, and what we may hope for in Christ. Faith and relationship to God in Christ means moving from lesser development to mature states of involvement with God and one another. It means moving from separation to relationship, away from those things which keep us from living a life of love and service, and toward our destination: living a life that is modelled after the life of God in Christ Jesus.

Consider the works of the early Fathers of the Church, those great theologians whose work still stands today as a pattern and guide for many believers' understanding of Christianity. In working out the doctrines we hold today, several theologians have explicitly treated the question of relationships between human development and religious development in the Christian faith. In his *Periphyseon, IV*, John Scotus Eriugena compares the Christian notion of paradise with a conception of maximal human development (Eriugena, 1995). Origen, Gregory of Nyssa, and Maximus the Confessor develop similar arguments. In their view, one cannot conceive of paradise (in the sense of the ful-filment of all creation) as independent from the question of what human life is for, toward what it might move, and human hopes for fulfilment in life. Irenaeus intertwines human criteria for assessing truth in the life of Jesus, the gospels, and tradition of the Church with scriptural reflections in order to illustrate what a theological concept of human development might look like. In his discussion of the possibility and nature of human progress, Irenaeus writes: 'And being newly created they are therefore childish and immature, and not fully prepared for an adult way of life' (Irenaeus, 1995). Irenaeus goes on to elaborate the parallel between God and a good mother, who knows in what measure to nourish her infant and has an overarching perspective of the infant that it cannot have of itself, in order that the infant may grow.

Both Origen and Tertullian address the inseparable relationship between the image of God, knowing God in Jesus Christ (i.e. human form), and our own understanding of what might become our best hope in growth and development. Origen puts it this way:

> This indicates that in his first creation man received the dignity of the image of God, but the fulfilment of the likeness is reserved for the final consummation; that is, he himself should obtain it by his own effort, through the imitation of God. The possibility of perfection given to him at the beginning by the dignity of the image, and then in the end, through the fulfilment of his works, should bring to perfect consummation the likeness of God. The Apostle John defines this state of things more clearly when he declares: 'My little children, we do not yet know what we shall be but if it shall be revealed to us concerning the Saviour, without doubt you will say: We shall be like him' (1 John 3:2). (Origen, 1995)

Such themes have continued to animate the work of theologians beyond those of the Church Fathers, moving through the arguments of the various Church Councils, the Reformation, right through to the beginnings of modernity and to the our postmodern or hypermodern period in the world. For example, reformers such as Calvin, Luther, and Hooker all took up the question of the relationship between salvation, development in God and human understandings of what life was for, toward what it was moving, and what its fulfilment might look like. Such concerns are also present in the works of the great modern theologians, such as Lonergan, Pannenberg, Bonhoeffer, Niebuhr, Tillich, Moltmann, Schillebeeckx, de Lubac, and others, and are lively questions in the theological works of contemporary theologians such as Dawn, Heyward, Milbank, Ward, Quash, Williams, Wells, Dormor, McDonald, Caddick, Morris, and Jenkins, to name but several current Anglican theologians. All of these theologians' works deserve reading in this light, but the case made by Timothy Jenkins is particularly interesting to us at the time of this writing.

Jenkins asserts that all churches and all their notions of salvation and goodness can be assessed in the relationship of freedom and order to what makes for human flourishing (Jenkins, 2005). For Jenkins, all religious groups have implicit and explicit notions of human flourishing that include notions of human development. His comments on Anglican ecclesiology are especially instructive, and serve to explain why the Church of England has found itself particularly taken up in a position of openness and dialogue with the human sciences. As a trained anthropologist as well as a priest and theologian, Jenkins' perspectives on anthropology and sociology might be usefully extended to how we could consider psychology as a contributor to our understanding of Jesus and the gospels. Another work of particular interest in this regard is the recent volume entitled *Psychology for Christian Ministry*, by Watts, Nye, and Savage (2002), showing how psychology can be useful in thinking about pastoral theology and the exercise of lay and ordained ministry.

Spiritual Direction, Jesus, and Human Development

One feature of the Christian faith is the tradition of spiritual direction, which is rooted in the sense of vocation described by St Paul in Ephesians 4:11–16, building upon the notion in the writings of the early Church that our task as Christians is to move in the image of God toward fulfilment in his likeness. Many authors, from those in the early years of the Church to more contemporary voices, describe how spiritual direction can help us see relationships between the psychology of human development and spiritual growth in Christ. In the Anglican tradition, this is evident in the Caroline Divines; in the Catholic tradition, in its emphasis on spiritual direction during the nine-teenth-century revival; and in the Evangelical tradition, in its appreciation of spiritual friendship. Twentieth-century advo-cates of spiritual direction include Evelyn Underhill, Father Andrew, Gilbert Shaw, Mother Mary Clare, and Reginald Som-erset Ward, but within the limited scope of this chapter we turn to the work of Margaret Guenther, priest in the Episcopal Church in the USA, and faculty member of the General Theo-logical Seminary in New York.

In her work, *Holy Listening* (Guenther, 1992), Guenther draws a nuanced picture of spiritual direction and the processes within, and the relationship between human developmental psychology and the concepts and goals of spiritual development in the Christian tradition. She is particularly effective in rooting the tradition in Scripture and in making characteristic depictions of Jesus. What she says about Jesus in this regard is apt for our appreciation of Jesus in the light of the psychology of human development. She notes that there are more than forty references to Jesus as teacher, in ways that accord with 'good practice' in the promotion of human development and spiritual growth.

Guenther finds the passage in the Gospel of St John 8:3–9, as we do, particularly useful in showing how Jesus taught some-times by silence, indirection, and by what we would call, in developmental terms, 'invitation rather than imposition'. In this passage, Jesus is asked by a group of Pharisees what they are to do with a woman taken in adultery. Refusing to be caught up in their references to Scripture, he writes in the sand on the ground, and says ' "Let anyone among you who is without sin be the first to throw a stone at her" '. Guenther cites another story from the same gospel of an encounter between Jesus and a woman (John 4:4–42); in this case the woman is a Samaritan. Jesus might have been expected by the religious authorities of his day to avoid her for social and cultural reasons, particularly since it seems she is 'tainted' by a long history of multiple sexual partners. However, Jesus refuses to condemn; instead he invites the woman to broaden her perspective, to trust her intuition that her destiny is a divinely authorised development in the image and towards the likeness of God. Rather than condemning, imposing direction, or communicating a message of 'from here on I will be watching you, tracking you, every step of the way ... and in the end I am going to get you, no matter what you do', he invites her onward, expressing trust in her basic dignity and in her desire to grow. 'Go, then, and sin no more,' he says. She is, and by extension we too are found by him, then given direction towards our destination, in order to grow into the fullness of our humanity and to the riches of life with God.

In the same spirit Guenther cites Amma Theodora, one of the few women spiritual teachers in the desert tradition, whose writing makes a profound link between developmental guidance and the pattern of Jesus in his ministry:

> A teacher ought to be a stranger to the desire for domination, vain-glory, and pride; one should not be able to fool him by flattery, nor blind him by gifts, nor conquer him by stomach, nor dominate him by anger, but he should be patient, gentle, humble as far as possible; he must be tested and without partisanship, full of concern, and a lover of souls. (cited in Ward, 1979, pp. 88–9)

This pattern of development implies a *process* of ever deepening one's relationship with God, and to know God intimately through patterning one's life after the life, attitudes, and behaviours of Jesus Christ. Parker Palmer (1986) brings together the weight of Christian tradition, the pattern of Jesus, and wisdom of human experience in an altogether fitting way:

> To know something or someone in truth is to enter troth with the known, to rejoin with new knowing what our minds have put asunder. To know in truth is to become betrothed, to engage the known with one's whole self, an engagement one enters with attentiveness, care, and good will. To know in truth is to allow one's self to be known as

well, to be vulnerable to the challenges and changes any true relationship brings. To know in truth is to enter into the life of that which we know and to allow it to enter into ours. Truthful knowing weds the knower and the known; even in separation, the two become part of each other's life and fate. (p. 31)

Conclusion

In this chapter we have traced some of the ways in which the psychology of human development has been concerned with the psychology of religious development. We have considered some caveats in any effort to 'apply' psychology to the understanding of religion, yet affirmed that within the Christian tradition there is reason to draw parallels between a psychological study of human religious development, and human/spiritual development as they are conceived in Scripture, in the person and pattern of Jesus, and in various forms of Christian theology and practice throughout history. In conclusion, if we may draw from both the psychology of human development and Christian theology as it pertains to Jesus and the gospels, we must acknowledge that we write at one fledgling and vulnerable point along the way. Our hope is to have made a small contribution to human growth and to meaningful witness regarding the bounty of the Christian tradition of which we are a part.

9

Leslie J. Francis

PSYCHOLOGICAL TYPES

Text and interpretation

Christian believers can approach the four gospels in a variety of
different ways. Preferred approaches have varied over time and
continue to vary today between different religious traditions,
orientations and denominations. What distinguishes the ways in
which many Christian believers approach the gospels from ways
in which non-believers approach the gospels is the deep conviction that these books constitute a special part in God's way of
communicating with the people of God. In this sense the four
gospels are, in one sense or another, concerned with divine
revelation.

On the basis of such beliefs about the nature of divine revelation, the Bible in general (and the gospels in particular) are
given a unique place in the Christian tradition and in Christian
liturgy and worship. This special status is demonstrated, for
example, in the Catholic liturgical tradition in which the gospel
reading is accorded a central role in the ministry of the word.
While the gospel is being read, the congregation stand as a sign
of respect and in recognition of the peculiar authority ascribed to

the gospel text. In this way the gospels are seen to be part of the living, dynamic and evolving Christian community.

As well as reading, listening to, and absorbing the text of the gospels, the Christian community has also long recognised and reflected on the responsibility of interpreting and of applying the text. At one level this activity of interpretation and application is embraced and engaged by individual Christians studying and mediating on the gospels in the privacy of their own personal lives. At another level this activity is embraced and engaged by Christians studying and celebrating together within the fellowship of the church through the formal acts of preaching and through the less formal encounters of bible-study groups.

Perhaps one of the most significant and impressive advances in biblical scholarship during the twentieth century concerned the growing importance attributed to taking seriously the perspective, standpoint or location of the reader in the art (or science) of biblical interpretation. Biblical interpretation, it is argued, is properly to be conceptualised as a dynamic dialogue between text and reader (where the reader may be seen as an individual or as a community, both of which in turn may be shaped by context). From this starting point a large literature has developed concerned with 'biblical hermeneutics', the dialogue between text and reader.

Initial concerns with taking seriously the perspective, standpoint or location of the reader in biblical hermeneutics were shaped much more strongly by sociological than by psychological perspectives. Broadly speaking, sociological perspectives are concentrated on those kinds of differences defined by social groups, while psychological perspectives concentrate on those kinds of differences defined by individuals. Early sociologically-shaped perspectives in biblical hermeneutics examined the influence on biblical interpretation of social factors like political power and economic oppression. Such perspectives gave rise to flourishing traditions like liberation theologies, feminist theologies and other contextual theologies, all of which carried profound implications for biblical interpretation. Among Christian believers the basic conviction holds good that this structured dialogue between the text of Scripture and the sociologically-defined location of the reader is central to the revelatory process of communication between God and the people of God.

Building on this established tradition of biblical hermeneutics pioneered through sociological perspectives, a more recent initiative has begun to establish the equally important insight that can be proposed to biblical hermeneutics by psychological perspectives. According to this initiative, taking the reader seriously means not only looking at the sociological location of the reader, but also at the psychological profile of the individual readers themselves. The branch of psychology that provides an exciting and challenging starting point for such engagement is concerned with 'individual differences'. Before examining a psychological approach to individual differences, however, it is crucial that this psychological approach should be properly underpinned by a theological evaluation of individual differences.

Theology of individual differences

A primary task of the theologian is to test the logic and internal coherence of all that the Church is teaching. A new psychological perspective on the interpretation of Scripture in general (and of the gospels in particular) would be highly suspect if such a perspective were not fully tested against (and integrated within) a coherent understanding of the major themes of Christian teaching as encapsulated, for example, by the key doctrines of creation, fall, salvation through the person of Christ, and sanctification through the work of the Holy Spirit.

The notion of individual differences is first and foremost grounded in a Christian doctrine of creation. The biblical basis for this doctrine of creation is informed by Genesis 1:27:

> God created humankind in God's image,
> in the image of God, God created them;
> male and female God created them.

The key insight provided by this biblical basis for a doctrine of creation is that God embraces diversity and that such diversity is reflected in those created in the image of God. The notion that God embraces diversity is clearly consistent with the Christian doctrine of Trinity and was also clearly anticipated within that strand in the opening books of the Old Testament which use a plural noun for God, as in Genesis 1:27.

In contrast with the narrative concerning Adam and Eve, a doctrine of creation grounded in Genesis 1:27 is committed theologically to recognising both men and women to be created equally in the image of God, and to arguing that individual differences that are created equal (male and female) need to be accorded equal value and equal status. If such a theology of individual differences hold good for sex differences then, by extension, such a theology should hold good also for other differences equally grounded in creation, that is to say in the intentionality of the divine creator. Such differences may well include those of ethnicity and those of personality. Before examining the implications of such a view, the Christian doctrine of creation needs to be set alongside the Christian doctrine of the fall.

The key point made by the Christian doctrine of the fall is that the image of the creator seen in the human creature is no longer unsullied. The image has been corrupted. The task to be undertaken by a sound theology of individual difference is to attempt to untangle those differences that can reasonably be posited to reflect the fall and those which persist as proper indicators of the image and of the intention of the divine creator. Those individual differences that reflect the corruption brought about by the fall must rightly be subject to the saving and transforming power of Christ (the doctrine of redemption) and the perfecting power of the Holy Spirit (the doctrine of sanctification). Those individual differences that reflect the divine image of the creator may need to be given proper respect and value in the hermeneutical dialogue between text and interpretation.

The individual differences of sex (male and female) may be

properly seen as reflecting creation rather than fall. As a consequence it becomes theologically inappropriate to call, say, on men to repent and to become women, or on women to repent and to become men. The argument seems equally strong to propose that the individual differences of ethnicity may be properly seen as reflecting creation rather than fall. Again, as a consequence, it becomes theologically inappropriate to call, say, on white people to repent and to become people of colour, or on people of colour to repent and to become white. There are, of course, enormous political implications that emerge from such a simple (and profound) theology of individual differences.

While the case may seem relatively clear-cut in respect of sex and ethnicity, the argument regarding individual differences in personality may prove to be somewhat more controversial. The problem arises, at least in part, from a real lack of clarity regarding ways in which the term personality itself can be used, especially in colloquial usage. The professional debate needs to be sharpened, therefore, by distinguishing between two related, but potentially very distinct terms: personality and character.

As generally employed within the psychology of individual differences, the term personality is reserved for those deep-seated individual differences that reflect something of the individual's genetic roots, while character reflects individual qualities that are nearer the surface. Qualities that define personality are largely immutable (like sex and ethnicity), while qualities that define character are open to change and to development. Qualities that define personality should be morally neutral and value free (like sex and ethnicity), while qualities that define character should be highly significant in terms of morality and personal values.

An example of individual differences in personality is provided by the well-understood distinction between introversion and extraversion. An example of individual differences in character is provided by the equally well-understood distinction between pride and humility. Both sets of differences may be illustrated by (and potentially confused by) a simple story related in Luke's gospel regarding Jesus' evaluation of and reaction to two men: a Pharisee and a tax-collector.

According to Luke 18:9–14, the Pharisee walked into the temple, stood up and prayed aloud about himself, thanking God that he was not a sinner like other people. The tax collector, by way of contrast, stood at a distance, not even looking up to heaven, and beat his breast, saying ' "God, be merciful to me, a sinner!" 'In terms of personality, the Pharisee seems to be displaying well-recognised characteristics of extraversion. He is behaving in a bold and socially engaging way. He is speaking out loud his thoughts and formulating them in a public context. By way of contrast, the tax-collector seems to be displaying well-recognised characteristics of introversion. He is behaving in a less socially confident manner. He is using a few well-chosen words that appear to have been rehearsed internally beforehand. In terms of character, the Pharisee seems to be displaying well-recognised characteristics of pride, even before his creator. By way of contrast, the tax-collector seems to be displaying well-recognised characteristics of humility, especially before his creator. The crucial point is that extraversion (personality) and pride (character) are two unrelated features of the Pharisee, just as introversion (personality) and humility (character) are two unrelated features of the tax-collector.

When Jesus affirmed the tax-collector as going away in the right relationship with God, Jesus affirmed his humility, not his predisposition for introversion. When Jesus reproved the Pharisee as going away in the wrong relationship with God, Jesus reproved his pride, not his predisposition for extraversion. The Christian gospel of repentance and forgiveness concerns the reformation of character, rather than the reformation of personality. It is theologically most appropriate to call on the Pharisee to repent of his sin of pride, to accept God's forgiveness and to grow in humility. However, it is theologically most inappropriate to call on the Pharisee to repent of his constitutional preference for extraversion and to struggle to become an introvert.

Psychology of individual differences

Generally speaking personality theory is concerned to identify and to assess those key individual differences at a psychological level which account for fundamental variation in human functioning and which are a consequence of innate disposition. As a relatively new science, it is hardly surprising that there are currently several different models of personality, developed from somewhat different starting-points, which both command broad respect and generate fierce debate among personality psychologists. Current theories of personality fall into two broad categories. One set of theories is concerned wholly with individual differences in normal personality. An example is provided by the distinction between sensing and intuition as measured by the Myers–Briggs Type Indicator. Neither sensing nor intuition is in any way associated with psychopathology. Another set of theories is concerned either with abnormal personality or with the continuity between normal and abnormal psychology. An example is provided by the continuum from tendermindedness, through toughmindedness, to psychoticism as measured by the Revised Eysenck Personality Questionnaire. High scores on this continuum are associated with psychotic disorders. In attempting to identify those innate human characteristics of personality of similar theological status to the characteristics of sex and ethnicity, the present analysis is concerned exclusively with those theories concerned wholly with individual differences in normal personality.

Different theories of normal personality have their own well-understood strengths and weaknesses. As in many scientific fields, different theories prove to be of different practical benefit within different arenas of application. The specific theory of normal personality and individual differences which has, to date, proved to be of most benefit in illuminating the process of biblical hermeneutics is the model of psychological type proposed by Carl Jung and made popular in both Christian and secular contexts, in a somewhat modified form, by the Myers–

Briggs Type Indicator. Jung's model of psychological type provided the intellectual basis for the SIFT method of biblical hermeneutics and of liturgical preaching developed by Bishop Peter Atkins (New Zealand) and Professor Leslie J. Francis (Wales) (see Francis and Atkins, 2000, 2001, 2002).

As popularised through books like *Gifts Differing* (Myers & Myers, 1980) and *Please Understand Me II* (Keirsey, 1998), psychological type theory distinguishes between four bipolar psychological perspectives: two orientations, two perceiving functions, two judging functions, and two attitudes.

The two orientations are concerned with where energy is drawn from and focused. On the one hand, extroverts are orientated towards the outer world; they are energised by the events and people around them. They enjoy communicating and thrive in stimulating and exciting environments. They tend to focus their attention upon what is happening outside themselves. They are usually open people, easy to get to know, and enjoy having many friends. On the other hand, introverts are orientated towards their inner world; they are energised by their inner ideas and concepts. They enjoy solitude, silence, and contemplation, as they tend to focus their attention upon what is happening in their inner life. They may prefer to have a small circle of intimate friends rather than many acquaintances.

The two perceiving functions are concerned with the way in which people perceive information. On the one hand, sensing types focus on the realities of a situation as perceived by the senses. They tend to focus on specific details, rather than the overall picture. They are concerned with the actual, the real, and the practical and tend to be down to earth and matter of fact. On the other hand, intuitive types focus on the possibilities of a situation, perceiving meanings and relationships. They may feel that perception by the senses is not as valuable as information gained from the unconscious mind as indirect associations and concepts impact on their perception. They focus on the overall picture, rather than on specific facts and data.

The two judging functions are concerned with the criteria

which people use to make decisions and judgements. On the one hand, thinking types make judgements based on objective, impersonal logic. They value integrity and justice. They are known for their truthfulness and for their desire for fairness. They consider conforming to principles to be of more importance than cultivating harmony. On the other hand, feeling types make judgements based on subjective, personal values. They value compassion and mercy. They are known for their tactfulness and for their desire for peace. They are more concerned to promote harmony, than to adhere to abstract principles.

The two attitudes towards the outer world are determined by which of the two sets of functions (that is, perceiving, or judging), is preferred in dealings with the outer world. On the one hand, judging types seek to order, rationalise, and structure their outer world, as they actively judge external stimuli. They enjoy routine and established patterns. They prefer to follow schedules in order to reach an established goal and may make use of lists, timetables, or diaries. They tend to be punctual, organised, and tidy. They prefer to make decisions quickly and to stick to their conclusions once made. On the other hand, perceiving types do not seek to impose order on the outer world, but are more reflective, perceptive, and open, as they passively perceive external stimuli. They have a flexible, open-ended approach to life. They enjoy change and spontaneity. They prefer to leave projects open in order to adapt and improve them. Their behaviour may often seem impulsive and unplanned.

Jung's view is that each individual develops one of the perceiving functions (sensing or intuition) at the expense of the other, and one of the judging functions (feeling or thinking) at the expense of the other. Moreover, for each individual the preferred perceiving function or the preferred judging function takes preference over the other, leading to the emergence of one dominant function that shapes the individual's dominant approach to life. Dominant sensing shapes the practical person. Dominant intuition shapes the imaginative person. Dominant feeling shapes the humane person. Dominant thinking shapes the analytic person.

It is a proper appreciation of the distinctive contribution of the four functions of sensing (S), intuition (I), feeling (F) and thinking (T) which shape the SIFT method of biblical hermeneutics and liturgical preaching (note that in much of the literature concerning psychological type, intuition is represented by N in order to reserve I to represent introversion. This general convention is not being followed in designation of the SIFT method). Each of the four functions approaches the text of Scripture in a distinctive way. Taken together, therefore, all four functions provide a much fuller and much richer set of insights into the text. Taken together, all four functions may get closer to fulfilling the dominical command to love the Lord your God ' "with all your mind" ' (Mark 12:30). It is important, therefore, to examine the distinctive characteristics of these four functions.

Sensing

Individuals who prefer sensing prefer to perceive information primarily through their five senses. They attend to practical and factual details, and are in touch with physical realities. They observe the small details of every day life and attend to actual experience. They prefer to let the eyes tell the mind.

Sensing types often have acute powers of observation, good memory for facts and details, the capacity for realism, and the ability to see the world as it is. They tend to rely on experience rather than theory and prefer to put their trust in what is known and in what has been well tried and tested.

Sensing types usually reach their conclusion step-by-step, observing each piece of information carefully. They are not easily inspired to interpret the information in front of them and they may not trust inspiration when it comes. They learn best about new ideas and theories through practical applications.

Intuition

Individuals who prefer intuition prefer to perceive information primarily by seeing patterns, meanings, and relationships. They tend to be good at reading between the lines and projecting possibilities for the future. They prefer to focus on the 'big picture'. They prefer to let the mind tell the eyes.

Intuitive types have the ability to see abstract, symbolic, and theoretical relationships, and the capacity to see future possibilities. They tend to put their reliance on inspiration rather than on past experience. They trust their intuitive grasp of meanings and relationships.

Individuals with a preference for intuition are aware of new challenges and possibilities. Their interest is in the new and untried. They are often discontent with the way things are and wish to improve them. They dislike doing the same thing repeatedly.

Feeling

Individuals who prefer feeling prefer to make decisions and judgements primarily based on subjective, personal values. They tend to place people, relationships, and interpersonal matters high on their agenda. They develop good skills at applying personal priorities. They are good at weighing human values and motives, both their own and other people's. They are characterised by qualities of empathy, sympathy, and trustfulness.

Feeling types like harmony and will work hard to bring about harmony between other people. They dislike telling other people unpleasant things or reprimanding other people. They take into account other people's feelings.

Feeling types are often sympathetic individuals. They take a great interest in the people behind the job and respond to other people's values as much as to their ideas. They enjoy pleasing people.

Thinking

Individuals who prefer thinking prefer to make decisions and judgements primarily based on objective, impersonal logic. They tend to place truth and reason high on their agenda. They often develop good powers of logical analysis. They tend to use objective and impersonal criteria in reaching decisions and to follow rationally the relationships between cause and effect. They may develop characteristics of being firm-minded and reasonable. They may sometimes appear sceptical.

Individuals with a preference for thinking tend to prize integrity, truthfulness, and fairness. They are usually able to put people in their place when they consider it necessary. They are able to take tough decisions and to reprimand others. They are also able to be firm and tough-minded about themselves.

Thinking types desire to be treated fairly and to see that other people are treated fairly as well. They are inclined to respond more to other people's ideas than to other people's feelings. They may inadvertently hurt other people's feelings without recognising that they are doing so.

Psychological type and the gospels

The SIFT method of biblical hermeneutics and liturgical preaching addresses to the gospel narrative in a systematic way the four sets of questions posed by the four psychological functions of sensing, intuition, feeling and thinking (Francis, 2003, 2005, 2006). The two perceiving functions (sensing and intuition) are applied first since the perceiving process is concerned with gathering information and ideas. The two judging functions (feeling and thinking) are then concerned with evaluating the information and ideas, since the judging process is concerned with the rational application of the information and the ideas gathered.

This chapter proposes to illustrate the SIFT method by starting right at the beginning of the gospel narrative, focusing on the birth narrative from Matthew. So now is the time to read

Matthew 2:1–12 and to reflect on your personal dialogue with the text of Scripture concerning the ancient eastern astrologers, the Magi, the wise men, which in turn gave rise to the tradition concerning three kings.

Sensing

The first step in the SIFT method is to address the sensing perspective. It is the sensing perspective that gets to grip with the text itself and which gives proper attention to the details of the passage and may wish to draw on insights of historic methods of biblical scholarship in order to draw in 'facts' from other parts of the Bible. The first set of questions asks, 'How does this passage speak to the sensing function? What are the facts and details? What is there to see, to hear, to touch, to smell, and to taste?'

When sensing types hear a passage of Scripture, they want to savour all the detail of the text and may become fascinated by descriptions that appeal to their senses. They tend to start from a fairly literal interest in what is being said. Sensing types may want to find out all they can about the passage and about the facts that stand behind the passage. They welcome preachers who lead them into the passage by repeating the story and by giving them time to observe and to appreciate the details. Sensing types quickly lose the thread if they are bombarded with too many possibilities too quickly.

The Matthean birth narrative provides plenty of details with which the sensing function can get to work. Picture the narrative as a five-act play. In the first act see the ancient eastern astrologers busy at their trade, watching, mapping and charting the heavenly bodies, planets, stars and comets. They are looking for patterns, significances and meanings. All their attention is caught by an unusually bright star. In act two the ancient eastern astrologers are travelling great distances, seeing new sights, meeting new people, before eventually exploring the historical, religious and political complexities of Jerusalem. In act three the ancient eastern astrologers incite the theologians and politicians of Jerusalem to search the Scriptures and to debate the political implications of a royal birth in the midst of Roman occupation and political instability. In act four the ancient eastern astrologers reach their real destination and meet with the infant Jesus and with Mary his mother. They bow down in adoration. See the gleaming gold; smell the fragrant frankincense; feel the embalming myrrh. In act five, see the ancient eastern astrologers ride off into the night by another route. See the Holy Family prepare for exile in Egypt. See the fury of the insecure Herod and hear the screams of the first victims of the Herodian infanticide. Here, indeed, is a five-act drama of dazzling proportions, epic implications, huge emotional significance, and profound theological complexity.

Intuition

The second step in the SIFT method is to address the intuitive perspective. It is the intuitive perspective that relates the biblical text to wider issues and concerns. The second set of questions asks, 'How does this passage speak to the intuitive function? What is there to speak to the imagination, to forge links with current situations, to illuminate issues in our lives?'

When intuitive types hear a passage of Scripture they want to know how that passage will fire their imagination and stimulate their ideas. They tend to focus not on the literal meaning of what is being said, but on the possibilities and challenges implied. Intuitive types may want to explore all of the possible directions in which the passage could lead. They welcome preachers who throw out suggestions and brainstorm possibilities, whether or not these are obviously linked to the passage, whether or not these ideas are followed through. Intuitive types quickly become bored with too much detail, too many facts and too much repetition.

The Matthean birth narrative provides so many jumping off points for the intuitive function. Take the star for example. These Magi glimpsed a distant far-off star. They only had a half-formed idea of what it meant or where it would lead. Yet they trusted their intuition; they set out on an evolving quest; they followed that star. In many ways their experience inspires a profound model of Christian discipleship. We, too, are attracted by the star of Christ. We must allow that star to guide our future. Or take the arrival in Jerusalem. The Magi turned up at the wrong place and asked the wrong questions of the wrong people. Yet they were doing what seemed sensible at the time. In our Christian discipleship we must be willing to take risks, to ask questions and to form the best judgements that we can. Or take the problematic gifts of mystic meaning. The Magi placed at the feet of Christ their gold and their wealth. So what are our material objectives; what do we plan to do with our wealth? The Magi placed at the feet of Christ their frankincense and their adoration. So what are our spiritual hopes and aims; what do we value most in life? The Magi placed at the feet of Christ their myrrh and their recognition of human mortality. So what do we hope to have achieved for God with our lives before we die?

Feeling

The third step in the SIFT method is to address the feeling perspective. It is the feeling perspective that examines the human interest in the biblical text and learns the lessons of God for harmonious and compassionate living. The third set of questions asks, 'How does this passage speak to the feeling function? What is there to speak about fundamental human values, about the relationships between people, and about what it is to be truly human?'

When feeling types hear a passage of Scripture they want to know what the passage has to say about personal values and about human relationships. They empathise deeply with people in the story and with the human drama in the narrative. Feeling types are keen to get inside the lives of people about whom they hear in Scripture. They want to explore what it felt like to be there at the time and how those feelings help to illuminate their Christian journey today. They welcome preachers who take time to develop the human dimension of the passage and who apply the passage to issues of compassion, harmony, and trust. Feeling types quickly lose interest in theological debates which explore abstract issues without clear application to personal relationships.

The Matthean birth narrative provides so much material to stimulate the feeling function. Put yourselves in the shoes of the wise men and examine what they really learnt from their experience about human life, about human values, and about the loving nature of God. Far from seeing themselves as wise men they must have seen themselves as really very foolish men. Imagine turning up in Jerusalem with such an ill-thought-through story. They had pinned their hopes on a star, but had no idea where the child was to be born. Imagine discovering how their naive question had so alarmed both the political and religious authorities. Imagine, worst of all, discovering how they had been so personally responsible for triggering Herod's brutal massacre of the innocent babies. All that sense of responsibility and sense of foolishness could have haunted those so-called wise men to the end of their days. Yet the gospel narrative ends on such a positive note. According to Matthew, the wise men returned by another route. They changed their minds, they faced in a new direction, and in Christian language they repented of their earlier plans. Here is the Christian promise of repentance, the promise of turning round and facing in a new direction. In light of God's infinite mercy and love these ancient eastern astrologers are remembered not for their foolishness but for their wisdom. So may the God who accepts and forgives, accept and forgive our foolishness and strengthen our wisdom in the service of the Kingdom of Christ.

Thinking

The fourth step in the SIFT method is to address the thinking perspective. It is the thinking perspective that examines the theological interest in the biblical text and which reflects rationally and crucially on issues of principle. The fourth set of questions asks, 'How does this passage speak to the thinking function? What is there to speak to the mind, to challenge us on issues of truth and justice, and to provoke profound theological thinking?'

When thinking types hear a passage of Scripture they want to know what the passage has to say about principles of truth and justice. They get caught up with the principles involved in the story and with the various kinds of truth claims being made. Thinking types are often keen to do theology and to follow through the implications and the logic of the positions they adopt. Some thinkers apply this perspective to a literal interpretation of Scripture, while other thinkers are more at home with the liberal interpretation of Scripture. They welcome preachers who are fully alert to the logical and to the theological implications of their themes. They value sermons that debate fundamental issues of integrity and righteousness. Thinking types quickly lose interest in sermons which concentrate on applications to personal relationships, but fail to debate critically issues of theology and morality.

The Matthean birth narrative provides so much material to stimulate the thinking function. At the level of New Testament scholarship there is the whole debate regarding the source of the basic narrative, its roots in Old Testament imagery, its central place in Matthew's distinctive theological perspective, and the extent to which the narrative may have been entirely shaped by Matthew for theological purposes. At the level of theological method there is the whole debate regarding the relationship between the different forms of knowledge and true theological insight into the nature and purposes of God. According to one account the ancient eastern astrologers could be seen as people concerned with the very secular (and somewhat suspect) science of astrology, or with a very secular form of philosophy, or with a developed religious tradition uninfluenced by the divine revelation of the Old Testament (certainly they seemed ignorant of the prophecies concerning Bethlehem). So immediately fundamental questions are being raised about the relationship between science and religion, about the relationship between different worldviews, and about the salvific value of non-Christian religious traditions.

Conclusion

The SIFT method of biblical hermeneutics and liturgical preaching has been displayed above in dialogue with Matthew 2:1–12. The same methodological principles can be applied to any gospel passage. The method has been grounded in three basic principles that involve taking seriously the perspective of the reader, the theology of individual differences, and the insights of psychological type. The method has been developed to help the people of God hear more clearly the divine revelation that emerges in the hermeneutical dialogue between the gospel text and the reader, preacher or listener. If this aim is achieved, then the link between psychology and faith, between psychologist and theologian has been well worthwhile.

10

Everett L. Worthington, Jr.

VIRTUE ORIENTATIONS

The Gospel is the good news. In fact, what is good is defined by the Gospel. Jesus is good. People are to be good by having the mind of Christ (Rom. 12:2), which presumably occurs in both a supernatural and more naturally worked-out transformation. People become oriented towards virtue as the Holy Spirit transforms them (Gal. 5:16–18), Christ lives in them (Col. 1:27), and the Father gives them grace, peace, and mercy (Eph. 1:2; Rom. 11:32).

In this chapter, I argue as follows. First, most people have (at least) two major orientations towards virtue, which I call *conscientiousness-based* and *warmth-based* virtue orientations (Worthington and Barry, 2005). We flip-flop between the two as we track through our flow of experiences. Yet we typically value one of the two virtue orientations more than the other – which can deflect us, at times, from true north. Second, I speculate about the brain science and psychology behind this valuing of the virtues. I hope to provide an account of the psychophysical basis for these orientations and the dominance of one orientation. (This does not stop God – or other spiritual beings – from deflecting the psychophysics periodically.) Third, I explore consequences of these virtue orientations on one's approach to three theological issues. These issues are (1) what one takes to be the central messages of Scripture, (2) one's orientation to a moral balance between justice and mercy, and (3) one's interpretation of passages that have historically tended to be controversial. In this chapter, I mostly am aimed at explicating the physical and psychological levels rather than writing from a theological point of view.

Virtue Orientations

Most of us believe that our judgements are balanced. It is others who are out of balance. Most Christians believe they hold a balanced orientation toward virtue (Reymond, 1998). Christians pursue virtue out of duty, responsibility, sense of accountability, love of truth, gratitude for God's grace and mercy, or love of God and God's creation. Each of the motivations takes precedence at various times due to exigencies of situations, memories that are triggered, associations that are made, or beliefs and values that are activated.

Identification of virtue orientations

Worthington *et al.* (2001) hypothesised two sets of virtues. Warmth-based virtues included love (the cardinal warmth-based virtue), empathy, sympathy, compassion, forgiveness, mercy, gratitude, grace, and humility. They were named 'warmth' because most entailed positive emotions that are warm and inviting. Conscientiousness-based motivations included self-control (the cardinal conscientiousness-based virtue), responsibility, accountability, duty, obligation, justice, and truth. They were named 'conscientiousness' because they focus on adherence to standards via an effort of will or self-control. Parenthetically, we later (Worthington and Barry, 2005) identified epistemic-based virtues, such as wisdom (the cardinal epistemic-based virtue), discernment, and knowledge, but for the present chapter, I will not further address epistemic virtue.

We identified eighteen classic virtues by surveying philosophical and religious literature. We then created scales that assessed warmth- and conscientiousness-based virtues using three methods, and factor analysed people's responses about preferences or likelihood of actually acting on these virtues. Overall, we found a first-order factor of virtue versus no-virtue. Some people simply endorsed the pursuit of virtue often, across many situations, over time; others did not. Within the virtues, we also found two secondary clusters: one of warmth-based and another of conscientiousness-based virtues. Thus, some people tended to endorse love, empathy, sympathy, forgiveness and other warmth-based virtues, but not as often endorse the conscientiousness-based virtues. Others tended to endorse conscientiousness-based virtues but less frequently, the warmth-based virtues. This has been true across a number of samples.

Does this accord with your experience? Some religions, like Christianity and Hindusim, are generally more valuing of warmth-based virtues. Others, like Judaism and Islam, are generally more valuing of conscientiousness-based virtues. However, there are clear differences *within* religions. In Christianity, for example, some denominations (e.g. Southern Baptists, Pentecostal Holiness, Reformed, Roman Catholicism) tend to value conscientiousness-based virtues more than warmth-based. Other denominations value warmth-based virtues more (notably United Methodists, Episcopalian or Anglicans, Presbyterian Church in the USA), and conscientiousness-based virtues less. It is important to note that while denominations may emphasise one set of virtue over another, they all value both sets.

In reality, most people do have a preference towards either warmth-based or conscientiousness-based virtues. One dominates, though both are usually considered to be important. People who highly endorse conscientiousness-based virtues will at times feel love, empathy, gratitude, forgiveness, mercy, and the like; conversely, people who highly endorse warmth-based virtues will at times feel a strong sense of duty, responsibility, and self control. Also, people do not tend to blend the virtues, but fluctuate between the two. At one time they may take one side, and at another time they may take the other.

The power of situations

What causes the fluctuations from applying a warmth-based virtue to a conscientiousness-based virtue? It could be many subtle factors; however, the strongest factors tend to make the most impact.

The situation in which we find ourselves often exerts more pressure on us than we would initially think. Stanley Milgram's classic study on conformity (Milgram, 1974) has shown that when we are placed in a situation where we need to obey an authority figure, we are likely to conform even if the instructions are out of line. In Milgram's study, he asked participants to administer high voltage electrical shocks to another person (a confederate) when he made a mistake in a learning task. In this type of situation, our attention is fixated on whether we are doing the right thing (i.e. obeying authority); the situation demands that we are conscientious and obedient. Milgram found that even when the instructions were apparently out of line (he asked participants to continue administering shocks even when the recipient of these shocks was screaming in pain), the presence of the authority is so powerful that it blocked people's ability to 'disobey'. Indeed, some participants in Milgram's study continued to administer electric shocks at lethal levels!

When these participants were interviewed, it became clear that they were focusing on doing a good job and being a good participant. Even though they were aware of the confederate's suffering and wanted to stop shocking him out of compassion, the majority of the subjects wanted to 'not spoil the experiment', not make trouble, and in some cases, get through the experiment quickly so they can actually help the confederate.

As Milgram's study showed, even the gentle presence of an authority figure makes the situation charged with the need to comply. The situation kept the participant's attention on the virtues of conscientiousness. It is possible that an intrusion can break through the intense focus (for example, a memory, one's Christian values, or Bible mandates), but these would have to be focused on intensely and sustained in order to override the already-strong focus on conscientiousness.

The role of emotions

Emotions inform people about the importance of situations, and emotions motivate actions (Damasio, 2000). Emotions put logical thinking out of focus, but focus our attention on survival issues. Emotional thinking occurs in a different part of the brain, as does logical analysis (Damasio, 2000), although the body as well as brain go together to make emotion. This difference in brain function is illustrated in another recent brain science experiment. Greene *et al.* (2001) posed a moral dilemma to a group of students. They were asked to decide whether they would *accidentally* kill one person in order to save five. About 80 percent of the people said they would pull the switch.

In a second scenario, these students were asked to make the same decision, but this time they were asked to decide whether they would *directly* kill one person in order to save five lives. In both scenarios, the action by the subject would result in one death and save five lives. The two problems are philosophically equivalent. However, in scenario two, only about 20 per cent of the subjects said they would push the stranger to his death.

Subjects were in functional MRI units as they thought through the dilemma. In the beginning of both scenarios, most neuronal activity was in the prefrontal cortex where logical analysis takes place. In the second scenario, however, when told they would have to directly kill a person, the neuronal activity moved primarily into the limbic system (the inner brain structures associated with emotional processing). The personal touch suddenly focused the person to a different type of thinking. Even though the philosophical problem was the same in both scenarios, most subjects were unwilling to solve the second problem with the same solution as the first. Their response to the situation was significantly affected by whether they were processing the problem logically and analytically or whether they were processing it emotionally.

To bring this back to virtue orientations, emotions seem to be associated with the switching on of warmth-based virtues such as compassion and mercy. Although the most of the students began by a logical analysis in the first scenario, the second scenario aroused their emotions so much so that the analysis was much more emotional. Thus, the presence of certain emotions can bring forth a person's warmth-based virtue orientation.

Genetic expression and learning

People differ in their emotional responsiveness, and such differences may be a part of their predisposition. Some are sensitive from birth and distinct patterns of emotional responsiveness show up soon after birth as temperaments (D. C. Rowe and Plomin, 1977). Studies on infants' temperament can reveal the nature of emotional responsiveness prior to socialisation and other environmental factors, and these predisposed individual differences can influence emotional and cognitive processing in later years.

Genetic endowment, of course, is only part of the picture. There are strong interactions between genetic expression and environment. A major aspect of an infant's environment is the parent–child relationship. Since children usually receive their genetic endowment from at least one parent, parent–child interactions foster the expression of genetic proclivity towards certain emotional responsiveness and expressions.

Now consider that a child might also have genetic markers that make it likely to be drawn to either conscientiousness-based virtues or warmth-based virtues. Furthermore, the parents – or at least one of them – are likely to have similar genetic endowment and thus likely to set up a home environment that fosters genetic expression of particular virtues.

People usually choose environments that complement their

genetic repertoire. This is seen in research showing that genetic heritability of traits increases as adults age and selectively choose environments in which they live (see Gilbert and Bailey, 2000). This self-selection of environments is not, however, possible for infants; parents decide for their children the type of environment in which they live. Even so, infant and parent still shape each other's behaviour. Thus, virtue orientation probably has a substantial heritability for infants, bolstered by parental environment.

As children age, they increasingly select their own environments (see Gilbert and Bailey, 2000). They interact more with peers of their own choosing, and their peers may have virtue orientations that are similar or different to their own. The typical teen is then endowed by nature and nurture to (1) have a preference for one cluster of virtues relative to the other and (2) have experiences that reinforce expression of virtues from each set.

As adolescents move to early and throughout adulthood, their environments become wider through their twenties and early thirties. The environments then tend to narrow as stable choices of mate, job or career, and leisure activities are made. As we can see in the lifespan, genetically predisposed virtue orientations are first reinforced during early childhood by the infant's parents. As children grow up and begin to make choices about their environments, social interactions may also encourage the development and expression of one virtue orientation over the other.

Applications of Virtue Orientations to Three Theological Issues

I have sketched a largely psychological model suggesting that two major orientations to virtue exist and is influenced and enforced by both nature and nurture. This has theological implications, which I will illustrate by examining how a person's virtue orientation might affect theological understanding of four topics mentioned earlier in the chapter – (1) the central message of Scripture, (2) one's understanding of Jesus, (3) one's understanding of the interplay of justice, mercy, grace, and forgiveness, and (4) one's interpretation of controversial passages.

Central messages of Scripture

Over the centuries, Christendom has been divided about the central messages in the Bible (Berkhof, 1996; Reymond, 1998). For example, Christians are saved by God's grace (i.e. an unmerited gift), which is appropriated by faith, and explicitly *not* by works (Eph. 2:8–9). Yet we are created by God to do good works, which God prepared in advance for us to do (Eph. 2:10). James 2:19–20 argues that faith is shown by works. This tension between faith, grace, and works inevitably has led people to differ on the centrality of grace, faith, and works.

We might speculate that people who are drawn to denominations and theologies that emphasise works are likely to favour a conscientiousness-based virtue orientation. Conversely, those who are drawn to denominations and theologies that emphasise grace may favour a warmth-based virtue orientation. The reverse direction of virtue orientation and church or theological preferences may also be found. Individuals whose characters tend to naturally express conscientiousness-based virtues may prefer churches that emphasise works over grace, while individuals who tend to naturally express warmth-based virtues may prefer churches that emphasise grace over works. Choice of environment and virtue orientation will thus likely reinforce each other to affect how the believer perceives and deals with these theological tensions.

Another tension in Scripture involves the emphasis on the passion and crucifixion of Jesus versus the resurrection and power of Jesus (Berkhof, 1996; Reymond, 1998). Roman Catholics predominantly emphasise the passion and meditate on the crucifix. Protestants have been drawn more to the empty tomb and the power of the resurrection. We might again speculate that Roman Catholics who more fervently embrace and consider the passion of Christ might be found high in the warmth-based virtues (e.g. empathy, sympathy, compassion). Protestants who emphasise God's power over Christ's suffering might more often value conscientiousness-based virtues such as truth and self-control.

Where does authority reside? Traditionally, some have emphasised the authority of leaders (e.g. Roman Catholics, the pope; Orthodoxy, the Councils; Anglicans, the archbishop; Presbyterians, elected representatives; Congregationalists, the members). Some have emphasised the authority of Scripture (e.g., the Reformers, Evangelical Protestants; Reymond, 1998). Some have emphasised the authority of tradition (e.g. Orthodoxy, Roman Catholicism, some Protestant mainline liturgical denominations). Some have emphasised the authority of identification with Christ (e.g., participationist traditions; non-denominational Protestant churches). We might hypothesise that concern over authority itself – those who value authority highly, regardless of its locus – might be associated with conscientiousness-based virtue. Depending on the locus of authority, specific conscientiousness-based virtues might be higher in one's hierarchy of virtues. For example, truth might be the cardinal virtue for staunchly Evangelical Protestants. Duty might be the cardinal virtue for Jesuits who pledge fealty to the Pope.

What qualities of God are most salient (Reymond, 1998)? Some see God as a loving, generous, compassionate father-figure; those people would probably value warmth-based virtues highly. Some see God as a stern demander of justice, law and righteousness; those people would probably value conscientiousness-based virtues.

Is God's written word primarily about righteousness and truth? Or is it more about grace, mercy and covenant?

Jack Haberer (2001), in *God Views: The convictions that drive us and divide us*, identified five views of God, which may have correlating virtue orientations. The confessionalist is most concerned with truth (i.e. conscientiousness-based virtue). The devotionalist is most concerned with a devoted connection with God (i.e. empathy and warmth-based virtues). The ecclesiast wants to nurture the church (i.e. a relational orientation that could emphasise either virtue orientation). The altruist is motivated by mercy and love for others (i.e. warmth-based virtues). The activist pursues social injustice (i.e. conscientiousness-based virtues).

Understanding Jesus' Life of Virtue

What qualities of Jesus does one emphasise (Berkhof, 1996)? For some, Jesus is seen mostly as a moral teacher who teaches right behaviour, morality, trust, and self-control – probably to those who value conscientiousness-based virtues highly. For others, Jesus is the embodiment of compassion, empathy, sympathy, and love – probably to those who value warmth-based virtues highly.

Most of the biblical texts to which I have referred throughout this chapter have been Pauline. Sometimes we get a different picture of Christianity when drawing from Pauline or gospel accounts alone. The entire New Testament canon is needed for an accurate theological perspective. Thus I have surveyed the synoptic gospels with only a little attention to John's gospel to inquire about the nature of virtue exhibited by Jesus. I have summarised categories of Jesus' acts in the table below. I then attempted to classify each general act as conscientiousness- or warmth-based virtue. Given my premise of the chapter, I acknowledge that my interpretation of the acts as conscientiousness-based or warmth-based might tell the reader more about *my judgement* than about Jesus. Nonetheless, my classification should provide an organization that allows others to make their own judgements.

Table: Jesus' Life of Virtue

Jesus' Act	Reference for Account	Primary Virtue Orientation
Begins ministry		
Struggles with temptation	Matt. 4:1–11; Mark 1:12–13; Luke 4:1–13	Conscientiousness
Seeks baptism	Matt. 3:13–17; Mark 1:9–11; Luke 3:21–2; John 1:31–4	Conscientiousness
Reads Scripture in the synagogue	Luke 4:14–30	Conscientiousness/ warmth
Chooses disciples	Matt. 4:18–22; Mark 1:16– 20; Luke 5:2–11; John 1:35–42 Matt. 9:9–13; Mark 2:14–17; Luke 5:27–32	Conscientiousness/ warmth
Teaches		
Teaches disciples	Matt. 12:36–52 Matt. 15:15–20; Mark 7:17– 23 Matt. 16: 13–16; Mark 8:27– 9; Luke 9:18–20 Matt. 16: 21–8; Mark 8:31— 9:1; Luke 9:22–7 Matt. 17:1–13; Mark 9:2–3; Luke 9:28–36 Matt. 17:19–23; Mark 9:28– 32 Matt. 17:25b–7 Matt. 18:1–5; Mark 9:33–7; Luke 9:46–8 Matt. 18:15–35 (forgiveness) Matt. 19:13–15; Mark 10:13– 16; Luke 18:15–17 Matt. 19:23—20:16	Conscientiousness/ warmth

	Matt. 20:17–19; Mark 10:32–4; Luke 18:31–3	
	Matt. 20:20–28; Mark 10:35–45	
	Matt. 21:18–22; Mark 11:12–14:20–24	
	Matt. 24:1–51; Mark 13:1–37; Luke 21:5–36	
	Matt. 25:1–13	
	Matt. 25:14–30; Luke 19:12–27	
	Matt. 25:31–46	
	Matt. 26:6–13; Mark 14:3–9; Luke 7:37–8; John 12:1–8	
	Matt. 26:17–29; Mark 14:12–25; Luke 22:7–13, 17–20	
	Matt. 26:31–5; Mark 14:27–31; Luke 22:31–4	
	Matt. 26:36–46; Mark 14:32–42; Luke 22:40–46	
	Matt. 28:1–8; Mark 16:1–8; Luke 24:1–10; John 20:1–8	
Discourses with strangers	Matt. 8:19–22; Luke 9:57–60	(Mostly) conscientiousness
	Matt. 9:14–17; Mark 2:18–22; Luke 5:33–9	
	Matt. 12:1–8; Mark 2:23–8; Luke 6:1–5	
	Matt. 12:9–14; Mark 3:1–6; Luke 6:6–11	
	Matt. 12:15–21	
	Matt. 13:1–34; Mark 4:1–34; Luke 8:4–15, 10:23–4	
	Matt. 19:16–29; Mark 10:17–30; Luke 18:18–30	
Mass lectures	Matt. 5:3—7:27; Luke 6:20–49	Conscientiousness
	Matt. 11:7–19; Luke 7:18–35	
	Matt. 12:46–50; Mark 3:31–5; Luke 8:19–21	
	Matt. 15:10–14; Mark 7:14–16	

	Matt. 17:14–19; Mark 9:14–28; Luke 9:37–42 Matt. 23:1–7; Mark 12:38–9; Luke 20:45–6 Matt. 23:37–9; Luke 13:34–5	
Eats with tax collectors and sinners	Matt. 9:9–13; Mark 2:14–17; Luke 5:27–32	Warmth
Passes judgement		
Pronounces judgements	*on unrepentant cities* Matt. 11:21–3; Luke 10:13–5 *on the fig tree* Matt. 21:18–22; Mark 11:12–14, 20–25 *on the Pharisees* *on spirits* *on unbelieving world* Matt. 18:6–9	Conscientiousness
Confronts and argues		
Argues with Pharisees (and Sadducees) and money changers	Matt. 12:24–45; Luke 11:24–32 Matt. 15:1–20; Mark 7:1–23 Matt. 16:1–2; Mark 8: 11–21 Matt. 19:1–9; Mark 10:1–12 Matt. 21:12–16; Mark 11:15–18; Luke 19:45–7 Matt. 21:23–7; Mark 11:27–33; Luke 20:1–8 Matt. 21:28–32 Matt. 21:33–46; Mark 12:1–12; Luke 20:9–19 Matt. 22:1–14; Luke 14:16–24 Matt. 22:15–22; Mark 12:13–17; Luke 20:20–26 Matt. 22:23–33; Mark 12:18–27; Luke 20:27–40 Matt. 22:34–40; Mark 12:28–31	Conscientiousness

	Matt. 22:41–6; Mark 12:35–7; Luke 20:41–4 Matt. 23:8–39 Matt. 26:47–56; Mark 14:43–50; Luke 22:47–53; Matt. 26:57–68; Mark 14:43–50; Luke 22:47–53 Matt. 26:57–68; Mark 14:53–65; John 18:12–13, 19–24	
Confronts Rome	Matt. 27:11–26; Mark 15:2–15; Luke 23:2–3, 18–25; John 18:29—19:16 Matt. 27:27–31; Mark 15:16–20 Matt. 27:33–44; Mark 15:22–32; Luke 23:33–45; John 19:17–24	Conscientiousness
Comforts		
Comforts	Matt. 11:28–30; Luke 10:21–2	Warmth
Forgives sins	Matt. 9:1–8; Mark 2:3–12; Luke 5:18–26	Warmth
Has compassion on crowds	Mark 10:36	Warmth
Does miracles		
Healing (n = 23)	*Those moved by compassion*	Warmth
Power over nature (n = 9)	*Those moved by truth* *Coin* Matt. 17:24–7 *Fig tree* Matt. 21:18–22, Mark 11:12–14, 20–25 *Walk on water* Matt. 14:25; Luke 6:48–51	Conscientiousness
Raising people from the dead (n = 3)	*Jairus' daughter* Matt. 9:18–19, 23–5; Mark 5:22–4, 38–42; Luke 8:41–2, 49–56 *Widow's son* Luke 7:11–15 *Lazarus* John 11:44	Warmth

Sends disciples to do works and signs		
Sends disciples to do works and signs	Matt. 10:2–4; Mark 3:16–19; Luke 6:4–16 Matt. 10:9–15; Mark 6:8–11; Luke 9:3–5, 10:4–12 Matt. 10:19–22; Mark 13:11–13; Luke 21:12–17 Matt. 10:26–33; Luke 12:2–9 Matt. 10:34–5; Luke 12:51–3	Warmth (see Matt. 10:36)

I identified seven major categories. For *Begins Ministry*, Jesus struggles with temptation, seeks baptism, and reads Scripture publicly to announce the commencement of his public ministry. Most acts are conscientiousness-based virtues. For *Teaches*, Jesus chooses and mentors his disciples, which could be considered a combination of warmth- and conscientiousness-based virtues. He also gives mass lectures (conscientiousness-based), has discourses with strangers (mostly conscientiousness-based), eats with outcasts and the unlovely, and comforts (mostly warmth-based). For *Confronts and Argues* and for *Passes Judgement*, Jesus' virtue orientation is almost exclusively conscientiousness-based. When Jesus *Comforts*, he is pursuing warmth-based virtues. When Jesus *Performs Miracles*, those involving healing, raising from the dead, and forgiving sins seem motivated by warmth-based virtue, while those involving demonstrating power over nature seem motivated by conscientiousness-based virtue. When Jesus *Sends his Disciples to Do Works and Signs*, those seem more motivated by warmth-based virtue than by conscientiousness.

By sheer magnitude of citation, Jesus seems more often oriented toward conscientiousness-based virtue than towards warmth-based virtue. However, both orientations to virtue are inarguably present and frequent.

Of course, the meanings and spiritual motivation of Jesus' virtuous behaviour are still debatable. One could easily portray Jesus' main purpose as being a moral exemplar and a moral teacher. To the contrary, one could conclude that Jesus' teaching on moral behaviour was meant to demonstrate human inadequacy at ever achieving moral perfection and the need for reliance in love on Jesus for all things. As Jesus said, ' "I am the vine; you are the branches. If a man remains in me and I in him, he will bear much fruit; apart from me you can do nothing" ' (John 15:5, NIV).

Let me reiterate important points before moving on. First, I have tried to be clear that these positions are all a matter of relative value, not exclusive bi-polar positions. Almost every Christian who is informed by Scripture will see Jesus *both* as a demanding moral teacher and as embodiment of love and grace. The relative value of each is what I am emphasising. Second, it is not a matter of finding one's immovable position on a static scale of virtues, arrayed from conscientiousness- to warmth-based virtues. Rather, people behave in one way today, the other tomorrow. It is the relative frequency with which one acts out one virtue or another which eventually establishes the orientation toward warmth or conscientiousness. These tendencies are by no means absolute.

Justice versus forgiveness, mercy, and grace

True Christian love includes justice, forgiveness, mercy, and grace (Evans, 2004). Sometimes love manifests in holding people accountable to sins of commission and omission. At other times, mercy is the watchword.

Love and justice are tied together through the experience of an injustice gap (Worthington, 2003). People keep an informal mental accounting of the amount of injustice that they perceive to still remain as a consequence of each transgression done to them. The injustice gap is the difference between the way a person would like to see an event (usually an unjust one) eventually resolved and the way it is perceived to be at present. Ease and likelihood of forgiveness is related to the size of the injustice gap, which may decrease when a person able to accept the situation, or perhaps when an apology has been offered.

Under the same conditions, individuals who have a conscientiousness-based value orientation are more likely to perceive injustices that an individual who is less concerned with justice, accountability, truth, and responsibility might simply overlook. Thus, a high conscientiousness-based virtue orientation should be expected to be more easily offended, perceive higher amounts of offence for a given transgression, and less willing to accept injustice and move on. The total amount of injustice from all people that is experienced by a person with a conscientiousness-based virtue orientation is likely to be greater than that of a person with a warmth-based virtue orientation, other things being equal.

A person high in warmth-based virtue orientation, on the other hand, would be more likely to be empathic, compassionate, sympathetic, and loving, and might be less likely to be offended (because he or she could better understand the point of view of the offender). The person high in warmth-based virtue orientation might also be more likely to emotionally forgive the offender if offence were taken. This is because emotional forgiveness is thought to occur through replacement of negative unforgiving emotions with positive other-oriented emotions.

A person's view of forgiveness and justice can affect the person's view of Scripture and the nature of God, as well as affecting the person's willingness to act in forgiveness or justice. For example, a person with a high orientation toward conscientiousness-based virtue will likely be oriented toward justice, and see God predominately as a just God. This person may see conscientiousness-based virtues, such as extending justice and truth to others, as more valuable and even more loving than warmth-based virtues. A person high in warmth-based virtue orientation will likely be oriented more toward forgiveness, mercy, and grace, and thus will be likely to emphasise God's attributes of mercy, grace and forgiveness in their interactions with others.

Interpretation of Controversial Passages

Let me take just one passage to illustrate how virtue orientations might affect the local biblical theology of a passage of Scripture. Ephesians 5:21—6:9, beginning with 'Be subject to one another out of reverence for Christ' is interpreted in a starkly different way by people in different theological traditions. I would suggest that to some extent, different virtue orientations might be behind the different interpretations.

Some people start their interpretation at Ephesians 5:22 and interpret the ensuing passages as instructions about God's order for relationships – between husbands and wives (wives submit to husbands; husbands love wives), parents and children (children obey parents; parents don't provoke children), and even masters and slaves (sometimes interpreted as employers and employees; employees honour employers; employers treat employees with respect). Other people begin the interpretation with verse 21, 'Be subject to one another'. Wives are exhorted to submit themselves to their husbands but husbands are to do likewise, laying down their lives for their wives, like Christ for the church. On one hand, the interpretation is about rules and structure – conscientiousness – and on the other hand it is about mutual self-giving and altruism – warmth. As we can see, these different interpretations of the same Scripture arise out of differing virtue orientations.

Conclusion

In the present chapter, I have argued that many aspects of theological interpretation come about because of some basic values people hold. I also have argued that these values are not merely socio-cultural, though culture clearly has an impact. Rather, I have suggested that perhaps these values might be rooted in individuals' genetic heritage, early child-rearing experiences, and fit of environment between child and parent as they mutually reinforce each other's behaviour. I have made this case also by speculating, based on some empirically based research into both brain science and social psychology, about the nature of psychological and physical processes that underlie the virtue orientations.

Rather than judging particular theological interpretations and the tensions that exist in Scripture's main message as right or wrong, it is perhaps more useful to understand these underlying orientations that influence biblical interpretation. In such mutually respectful striving, perhaps acrimony within various traditions of Christianity might be lessened. Although virtue orientations are stable, they are also fluid. Thus it is more constructive to acknowledge these different virtue orientations, both of which are valued in Scripture, and to accept that one may be emphasised over the other because of the predispositions of people belonging to different denominations and adhering to different theologies. Emphasising only one virtue orientation without also recognising or appreciating the other makes for an incomplete and distorted theology.

References

Ainsworth, M. 1982. 'Attachment: Retrospect and prospect' in C. M. Parkes and J. Stevenson-Hinde (eds.), *The Place of Attachment in Human Behaviour*, pp. 3–30. New York, Basic Books.

Anderson, P. N. 1997. *The Christology of the Fourth Gospel: Its unity and disunity in the light of John 6*. Valley Forge, Trinity Press International.

Axelrod, R. 1984. *The Evolution of Cooperation*. New York, Basic Books.

Badcock, C. R. 2000. *Evolutionary Psychology: A critical introduction*. Oxford, Blackwell.

Batson, C. D., Shoenrade, P., and Ventis, W. L. 1993. *Religion and the Individual: A social-psychological perspective*. New York, Oxford University Press.

Beck, A. T. 1976. *Cognitive Therapy and the Emotional Disorders*. New York, International Universities Press.

Beck, A. T. 1993. 'Cognitive therapy: Past, present and future', *Journal of Consulting and Clinical Psychology, 61*(2), 194–8.

Beck, J. R. 1998. Review of 'Jesus at thirty: A psychological and historical portrait', *Denver Journal: An online review of current biblical and theological studies, 1*, 0702. Retrieved 15 January 2006 from www.denverseminary.edu/dj/articles1998/0700/0702.php.

Berger, K. 2003. *Identity and Experience in the New Testament*. Minneapolis, MN, Augsberg Fortress Press.

Berkhof, L. 1996. *Systematic Theology*. Grand Rapids, MI, Eerdmans.

Berry, J. W., Poortinga, Y. H., Segall, M. H., and Dasen, P. R. 1992. *Cross-cultural Psychology: Research and applications*. Cambridge, Cambridge University Press.

Bornkamm, G. 1960. *Jesus of Nazareth*. London, Hodder & Stoughton.

Bowlby, J. 1969. *Attachment*, vol. 1. New York, Basic Books.

Bowlby, J. 1980. *Loss: Sadness and depression*, vol. 3. New York, Basic Books.

Browne, D. 1997. 'Film, movies, meanings' in C. Marsh and G. Ortiz (eds.), *Explorations in Theology and Film*, pp. 9–20. Oxford, Blackwell.

Bryant, C. 1983. *Jung and the Christian Way*. London, Darton, Longman & Todd.

Burke, P. 1992. *History and Social Theory*. Ithaca, NY, Cornell University Press.

Cadbury, H. J. 1937. *The Peril of Modernizing Jesus*. London, Macmillan.

Capps, D. 2000. *Jesus: A Psychological Biography*. St Louis, Chalice Press.

Capps, D. 2004. 'A psychobiography of Jesus' in J. H. Ellens and W. G. Rollins (eds.), *Psychology and the Bible*. Westport, CT, Greenwood.

Carter, S. 1963. 'Lord of the dance', song lyrics. London, Stainer & Bell.

Childs, H. 2000. *The Myth of the Historical Jesus and the Evolution of Consciousness*. Atlanta, Society of Biblical Literature Dissertation Series.

Crossan, J. D. 1991. *The Historical Jesus: The life of a mediterranean Jewish peasant*. Edinburgh, T&T Clark.

Damasio, A. 2000. *The Feeling of what Happens: Body and emotion in the making of consciousness*. New York, Harvest Books.

Day, J. 1993. 'Speaking of belief: Language, performance, and narrative in the psychology of religion, *International Journal for the Psychology of Religion*, 3(4), 213–30.

Day, J. 2000. 'Le discours religieux en contexte: Deux études auprès d'adolescents et de jeunes adultes in Belgique francophone' in V. Saroglou and D. Hutsebaut (eds.), *Religion et Développement Humain: Questions psychologiques*, pp. 57–69. Paris, L'Harmatton.

Day, J. 2001. 'From structuralism to eternity?: Re-imagining the psychology of religious development after the cognitive-developmental paradigm', *International Journal for the Psychology of Religion*, 11, 173–83.

Day, J. 2002. 'Religious development as discursive construction' in C. Hermans, G. Immink, A. de Jong and J. van der Lans (eds.), *Social Construction and Theology*. Boston, Brill.

Day, J. 2006a, August. 'Cultural differences in moral and religious reasoning amongst Christian and Muslim youth in Belgium and England', paper presented at the International Association for Psychology of Religion Triennial Congress. Lueven.

Day, J. 2006b, April. 'Religious elements in moral decision-making: Empirical studies of Christian and Muslim adolescents and young adults in Belgium and England', paper presented at the Annual Conference for the Society for Research in Adult Development. San Francisco.

Day, J. in press. 'Conscience: Does religion matter? Empirical studies of religious elements in pro-social behaviour, prejudice, empathy development, and moral decision-making' in W. Koop (ed.), *The Structure and Development of Conscience*. London, Psychology Press.

Day, J., and Naedts, M. 1999. 'Religious development' in R. Mosher, D. Youngman and J. M. Day (eds.), *Human Development across the Lifespan: Educational and psychological applications*, pp. 239–64. Westport, CT, Praeger Publishing.

Day, J., and Tappan, M. 1996. 'The narrative approach to moral development: From the epistemic subject to dialogical selves', *Human Development, 39*(2), 67–82.

Day, J., and Youngman, D. 2003. 'Discursive practices and their interpretation in the psychology of religious development: From constructivist canons to constructionist alternatives' in J. Demmick and C. Andreoletti (eds.), *The Handbook of Adult Development*, New York, Plenum.

Degelman, D., Mullen, P., and Mullen, N. 1984. 'Development of abstract thinking: A comparison of Roman Catholic and Nazarene youth', *Journal of Psychology and Christianity, 3*, 44–9.

Dominian, J. 1998. *One Like Us: Psychological interpretation of Jesus*. London, Darton, Longman and Todd.

Dunn, J. D. G. 2003. *Jesus Remembered*. Cambridge, Eerdmans.

Edinger, E. F. 1972. *Ego and Archetype: Individuation and the religious function of the psyche*. New York, Putnam.

Ehrman, B. 2005. 'Did Jesus get angry or agonize? A text critic pursues the Jesus story', *Bible Review, 21*, 17–26, 49.

Elkind, D. 1964. 'Piaget's semi-clinical interview and the study of spontaneous religion', *Journal for the Scientific Study of Religion, 4*, 40–46.

Ellens, J. H., and Rollins, W. G. 2004. *Psychology and the Bible: A new way to read the scriptures*. Westport, Praeger.

Erikson, E. 1958. *Young Man Luther: A study in psychoanalysis and history*. London, Faber.

Erikson, E. 1981. 'The Galilean sayings and the sense of "I"', *Yale Review, 70*, 321–62.

Eriugena, J. S. 1995. 'Periphyseon, IV, 15' in A. McGrath (ed.), *The Christian Theology Reader*, 1st edn. Oxford, Blackwell.

Evans, C. S. 2004. *Kierkegaard's Ethic of Love: Divine Commands and Moral Obligations*. New York, Oxford University Press.

Ford, R. Q. 1997. *The Parables of Jesus: Recovering the art of listening*. Minneapolis, MN, Augsberg Fortress Press.

Fowler, J. 1981. *Stages of Faith*. San Francisco, Harper & Row.

Fowler, J. 1994. *Faithful Change*. San Francisco, Harper & Row.

Francis, L. J. 1997. *Personality Type and Scripture: Exploring Mark's gospel.* London, Mowbray.

Francis, L. J. 2003. 'Psychological type and biblical hermeneutics: SIFT method of preaching', *Rural Theology, 1,* 13–23.

Francis, L. J. 2005. *Faith and Psychology: Personality, religion and the individual.* London, Darton, Longman & Todd.

Francis, L. J. 2006. 'Psychological type and liturgical preaching: the SIFT method', *Liturgy,* Vol. 21, no. 3, 11–20.

Francis, L. J., and Atkins, P. 2000. *Exploring Luke's Gospel: A guide to the gospel readings in the Revised Common Lectionary.* London, Mowbray.

Francis, L. J., and Atkins, P. 2001. *Exploring Matthew's Gospel: A guide to the gospel readings in the Revised Common Lectionary.* London, Mowbray.

Francis, L. J., and Atkins, P. 2002. *Exploring Mark's Gospel: An aid for readers and preachers using year B of the Revised Common Lectionary.* London, Continuum.

Ganzevoort, R. 1998a. 'De praxis als verhaal: Introductie op een narratief perspectief' in *De praxis als verhaal: Narrativiteit en praktische theologie.* Kampen, Uitgeverij Kok.

Ganzevoort, R. (ed.). 1998b. *De praxis als verhaal: Narrativiteit en praktische theologie.* Kampen, Uitgeverij Kok.

Gay, P. 1985. *Freud for Historians.* Oxford, Oxford University Press.

Gergen, K. 1994. *Realities and Relationships: Soundings in social construction.* Cambridge, MA, Harvard University Press.

Gibson, M. (director), B. Davey, M. Gibson, S. McEveety and E. Sisti (producers). 2004. *The Passion of the Christ,* film. United States, Newmarket Films.

Gilbert, P., and Bailey, K. G. (eds.). 2000. *Genes on the Couch: Explorations in evolutionary psychology.* Philadelphia, Routledge.

Goldman, R. 1964. *Religious Thinking from Childhood to Adolescence.* New York, Seabury Press.

Graham, D. J. 1997. 'The uses of film in theology' in C. Marsh and G. Ortiz (eds.), *Explorations in Theology and Film* (pp. 35–44). Oxford, Blackwell.

Granqvist, P. 2002. 'Attachment and religiosity in adolescence: Cross-sectional and longitudinal evaluations', *Personality and Social Psychology Bulletin, 28,* 260–70.

Greene, J. D., Sommerville, R. B., Nystrom, L. E., Darley, J. M., and Cohen, J. D. 2001. 'An fMRI investigation of emotional engagement in moral judgment', *Science, 293,* 2105–8.

Guenther, M. 1992. *Holy Listening: The art of spiritual direction.* Cambridge, MA, Cowley Publications.

Haberer, J. H., Jr. 2001. *God Views: The convictions that drive us and divide us*. Louisville, KY, Geneva Press.

Haley, J. 1989. *The Power Tactics of Jesus Christ and Other Essays*, 2nd edn. London, W. W. Norton.

Hall, G. S. 1917. *Jesus the Christ in the Light of Psychology*. New York, Doubleday.

Horrell, D. R. 1999. *Social-scientific Approaches to the Interpretation of the New Testament*. Edinburgh, T&T Clark.

Irenaeus. 1995. 'adversus haereses, IV.xxxviii.1', in A. McGrath (ed.), *The Christian Theology Reader*, 1st edn. Oxford, Blackwell.

Jenkins, T. 2005. 'Anglicanism: the only answer to modernity' in D. Dormor, J. McDonald and J. Caddick (eds.), *Anglicanism: The answer to modernity*. London, Continuum International.

Jewison, N. (director), N. Jewison and R. Stigwood (producers). 1973. *Jesus Christ Superstar*, film. United States, Universal Pictures.

Johnson, C. B. 1983. *The Psychology of Biblical Interpretation*. Grand Rapids, MI, Zondervan.

Jung, C. G. 1954. *Answer to Job*. London, Routledge & Kegan Paul.

Kazantzakis, N. 1998. *The Last Temptation of Christ*. New York, Simon & Schuster.

Keirsey, D. 1998. *Please Understand Me II: Temperament, character, intelligence*. Del Mar, CA, Promethus Nemesis.

Kelly, G. A. 1991. *A Theory of Personality*, vol. 1. London, Routledge.

Kirkpatrick, L. 1997. 'A longitudinal study of changes in religious belief and behaviour as a function of individual differences in attachment style', *Journal for the Scientific Study of Religion*, 36, 207–17.

Kirkpatrick, L., and Shaver, P. 1990. 'Attachment theory and religion: Childhood attachments, religious beliefs, and conversion', *Journal for the Scientific Study of Religion*, 29, 315–34.

Kunkel, F. 1987. *Creation Continues: Psychological interpretation of the gospel of Matthew*. New York, Paulist Press.

Levinson, D. 1978. *The Seasons of a Man's Life*. New York, Knopf.

Maier, S. F. & Seligman, M. E. D. 1976. *Learned Helplessness: Theory and Evidence*. Journal of Experimental Psychology, 105(1): 3–46.

Malina, B. J., and Neyrey, J. H. 1996. *Portraits of Paul: An archaeology of ancient personality*. Louisville, KY, Westminster John Knox Press.

Maslow, A. H. 1964. *Religions, Values and Peak Experiences*. Columbus, OH, Ohio State University Press.

McGann, D. 1985. *The Journeying Self: The gospel of Mark through a Jungian perspective*. New York, Paulist Press.

McGann, D. 1988. *Journeying within Transcendence: The gospel of John through a Jungian perspective*. New York, Paulist Press.

McGrath, A. (ed.). 1995. *The Christian Theology Reader*, 1st edn. Oxford, Blackwell.

McIntyre, J. 1998. *The Shape of Christology: Studies in the doctrine of the person of Christ*. Edinburgh, T&T Clark.

Meier, J. B. 1994. *Mentor, Message, and Miracles*, vol. 2. New York, Doubleday.

Meier, J. B. 1999. 'The present state of the third quest for the historical Jesus: Loss and gain', *Biblica, 80*, 459–87.

Meyer, B. F. 1994. 'Jesus' ministry and self-understanding' in B. Chilton and C. Evans (eds.), *Studying the Historical Jesus: Evaluations of the state of current research*, pp. 337–52. Leiden, E. J. Brill.

Milgram, S. 1974. *Obedience to Authority*. New York, Harper & Row.

Miller, J. W. 1997. *Jesus at Thirty: A psychological and historical portrait*. Minneapolis, MN, Augsberg Fortress Press.

Myers, I. B., and Myers, P. B. 1980. *Gifts Differing: Understanding personality type*. Palo Alto, CA, Consulting Psychologists Press.

Newheart, M. W. 2001. *Word and Soul: A psychological, literary and cultural reading of the fourth gospel*. Collegeville, MN, Liturgical Press.

Nissinen, M. 1998. *Homoeroticism in the Biblical World*. Minneapolis, MN, Augsberg Fortress Press.

Origen. 1995. 'de principiis, III.iv.1' in A. McGrath (ed.), *The Christian Theology Reader*, 1st edn, pp. 214. Oxford, Blackwell.

Oser, F., and Reich, H. (eds.). 1996. *Eingebettet ins Menschein: Beispiel Religion: Aktuelle psychologische studien zur entwicklung von religiosität*. Lengerich. Pabst Scientific.

Palmer, P. 1986. *To Know as we are Known: Education as a spiritual journey*. San Francisco, Harper & Row.

Peatling, J., and Labbs, C. 1975. 'Cognitive development in pupils in grades four through twelve: The incidence of concrete and abstract and religious thinking', *Character Potential: A record of research, 7*, 107–15.

Pruyser, P. W. 1991. 'Anxiety, guilt, and shame in the atonement' in H. N. Malony and B. Spilka (eds.), *Religion in Psychodynamic Perspective: The contributions of Paul W. Pruyser*. New York, Oxford University Press.

Reymond, R. L. 1998. *A New Systematic Theology of the Christian Faith*. Nashville, Nelson.

Rogers, C. R. 1951. *Client-centered Counselling*. Boston, Houghton-Mifflin.

Rollins, W. G. 1999. *Soul and Psyche: The Bible in psychological perspective*. Minneapolis, MN, Augsberg Fortress Press.

Rowe, D. 1987. *Beyond Fear*. London, Fontana.

Rowe, D. C., and Plomin, R. 1977. 'Temperament in early childhood', *Journal of Personality Assessment, 41*, 150-56.

Sanders, E. P. 1985. *Jesus and Judaism*. London, SCM-Canterbury Press.

Sanford, J. A. 1987. *The Kingdom Within: The inner meaning of Jesus' sayings*. San Francisco, Harper & Row.

Sanford, J. A. 1993. *Mystical Christianity: A psychological commentary on the gospel of John*. New York, Crossroad Publishing.

Saroglou, V. 2001. 'La religion des jeunes et leur personnalité: Études récentes en Belgique francophone' in V. Saroglou and D. Hutsebaut (eds.), *Religion et Développement Humain Questions psychologiques*. Paris, L'Harmattan.

Schweitzer, A. 1913/1948. *The Psychiatric Study of Jesus,* trans. C. R. Roy. Boston, Beacon Press.

Scorsese, M. (director), B. De Fina and H. Ufland (producers). 1988. *The Last Temptation of Christ*, film. United States, Universal Pictures.

Snaith, N. H. 1975. 'Leviticus' in M. Black (ed.), *Peake's Commentary on the Bible*. London, Nelson.

Spilka, B., Hood, R. W., Jr., Hunsberger, B., and Gorsuch, R. 2003. *The Psychology of Religion: An empirical approach*. New York, The Guilford Press.

Spilka, B., and Malony, H. N. (eds.). 1991. *Religion in Psychodynamic Perspective: The contributions of Paul W. Pruyser*. New York, Oxford University Press.

Stampfl, T. G., and Lewis, D. J. 1967. 'Essentials of implosive therapy: A learning–theory-based psychodynamic behaviour therapy', *Journal of Abnormal Psychology, 72*, 496–503.

Streib, H. 1991. *Hermeneutics of Symbol, Metaphor, and Narrative in Faith Development Theory*. Frankfurt, Peter Lang.

Streib, H. 1997. 'Religion als stilfrage. Zur Revision struktureller Differenzierung von Religion im Blick auf die Analyse der pluralistisch-religiösenlage der gegenwart', *Archiv für Religionspsychologie, 22*, 48–69.

Szaluta, J. 1999. *Psychohistory: Theory and practice*. New York, Peter Lang.

Tamminen, K., and Nurmi, K. 1995. 'Developmental theory and religious experience' in R. W. Hood, Jr. (ed.), *Handbook of Religious Experience*. Birmingham, AL, Religious Education Press.

Telford, W. R. 1997. 'Jesus Christ movie star: The depiction of Jesus in the cinema' in C. Marsh and G. Ortiz (eds.), *Explorations in Theology and Film* (pp. 115–40). Oxford, Blackwell.

Telford, W. R. 1998. 'Review of Jesus at thirty: A psychological and historical portrait', *Review of Biblical Literature*. Retrieved 15 January

2006 from www.bookreviews.org/bookdetail.asp?TitleId=78& CodePage=78.

Theissen, G. 1987. *Psychological Aspects of Pauline Theology*. Edinburgh, T&T Clark.

Theissen, G., Winter, D., and Boring, M. E. 2002. *The Quest for the Plausible Jesus: The question of criteria*. Louisville, KY, Westminster John Knox.

Ullmann, L. P., and Krasner, L. 1965. *Case Studies in Behaviour Modification*. New York, Holt, Rheinhart & Winston.

Vitz, P. C. 1977. *Psychology as Religion*. Grand Rapids, MI, Eerdmans.

Ward, B. 1979. *The Sayings of the Desert Fathers*. London, Mowbray.

Watts, F. N. 2001. 'Shame, sin and guilt' in A. McFadyen and M. Sarot (eds.), *Forgiveness and Truth: Explorations in contemporary theology*. Edinburgh, T&T Clark.

Watts, F. N. in press. 'Personal transformation: Perspectives from psychology and Christianity' in P. Hefner and J. D. Koss-Chioino (eds.), *Spiritual Transformation and Healing*. Walnut Creek, CA, Altamira Press.

Watts, F. N., Nye, R., and Savage, S. B. 2002. *Psychology for Christian Ministry*. London, Routledge.

Witherington, B. I. 1997. *The Jesus Quest: The third search for the Jew of Nazareth*, 2nd edn. Leicester, InterVarsity Press.

Wolpe, J. 1969. 'Basic principles and practices of behaviour therapy of neuroses', *American Journal of Psychiatry*, 125, 1242–7.

Worthington, E. L., Jr. 2003. *Forgiving and Reconciling: Bridges to Wholeness and Hope*. Downers Grove, IL, InterVarsity Press.

Worthington, E. L., Jr., and Barry, J. W. 2005. 'Character development, virtues, and vices' in W. R. Miller and H. D. Delaney (eds.), *Human Nature, Motivation, and Change: Judeo-Christian perspectives on psychology* (pp. 145–64). Washington, DC, American Psychological Association.

Worthington, E. L., Jr., Berry, J. W., and Parrott, L. I. 2001. 'Unforgiveness, forgiveness, religion, and health' in T. G. Plante and A. Sherman (eds.), *Faith and Health: Psychological perspectives*, pp. 107–38. New York, Guilford.

Wright, N. T. 1996. *Jesus and the Victory of God*. London, SPCK.

Index